Divine Appointments

Igniting Your Passion to
Fulfill Your Destiny

Larry Tomczak

Treasure House

An Imprint of
Destiny Image® Publishers, Inc.
P.O. Box 310
Shippensburg, PA 17257-0310

"For where your treasure is,
there will your heart be also." Matthew 6:21

ISBN 1-56043-320-5
(Previously published under ISBN 0-89283-261-4 by Vine Books)

For Worldwide Distribution
Printed in the U.S.A.

This book and all other Destiny Image, Revival Press, and Treasure House books are available at Christian bookstores and distributors worldwide.

For a U.S. bookstore nearest you, call **1-800-722-6774**.
For more information on foreign distributors, call **717-532-3040**.
Or reach us on the Internet: **http://www.reapernet.com**

This book is dedicated to my seventy-four-year-old mother, Sophie, who to this day continues to invest in me so that I in turn can invest in others. Without her love and example I would not be the man of God that I am today. When Dad passed away just a few months ago, God arranged a divine appointment for her: I needed a quiet place to write this book, and she needed the reassuring presence of her only son. How providential that I could use her upstairs bedroom for writing, be available to chat during breaks, and simply enjoy being with her during the crafting of this labor of love.

"Out of the deeds of love done today come the destinies of tomorrow."

Contents

Foreword

Recently I interviewed one of America's richest and most successful businessmen. I asked him the secret of his success.

"Some people inherit success," he said. "Others steal it or obtain it by running over their competitors. I became successful by being in the right place at the right time."

The world calls that *luck*, or *good fortune*. And, I guess, chance does play a role with some people.

But when a man or woman commits his life to Jesus Christ, he is no longer at the mercy of chance or fate. No longer does he have to wish for good luck—or fear missing an opportunity. The person living under the lordship of Jesus Christ is controlled by his Spirit, just as surely (indeed, far more surely) as the brain controls the automatic functions of the body.

This book shows how you can, by programming life to be in harmony with God's Spirit, always be at the right place at the right time. Larry Tomczak has not only written about this concept in an exciting way—he lives it out in an exciting lifestyle. In these pages he shares some of those incredible stories—how by hearing and obeying he "just happened" to be in time for God's appointment. At times he was God's messenger. At other times he was God's answer to someone else's prayer. At all times he was God's man for the situation.

The result: success.

And so with you. Every day can become a masterpiece for God.

—Jamie Buckingham (1932–1992)
Palm Bay, Florida
Author, Former Editor of *Leadership Today*
Columnist of "Final Word"

Part I

Your Divine Appointment with Destiny

Before I formed you in the womb I knew you, and appointed you a prophet to the nations. (Jer 1:5)

ONE

Why Am I Here?

"ONE BULLET TO THE HEART," I thought, "and it will all be over."

It was late on a Friday evening. Only a few minutes before, I had been standing on the curb of Euclid Avenue, a busy, well-lit street near the campus of Cleveland State University, in the heart of the downtown area. My destination was also near Euclid Avenue, but about ninety blocks away. Since my car was in the shop, I had been forced to hitchhike.

I often hitched rides in this part of town and had never had any problems. In fact, just a few months before, I had been picked up in the middle of a driving rainstorm by an elderly black pastor who had invited me to visit his church. It was there I first heard about accepting Jesus Christ into my life as my personal Lord and Savior. I had subsequently committed my life to Christ, and now, only a few weeks later and entering my senior year of college, I was on my way to a retreat to learn more about being his disciple. Getting there, I was about to discover, was definitely not going to be half the fun.

"Where ya headed, kid?"

The voice came from inside a rusty, dented Oldsmobile, through a partially opened door.

"Euclid and 130th," I replied.

"Get in."

I did. Three young guys sat in the car. They appeared to be in their mid-twenties. They also looked like pretty tough customers.

"Thanks for stopping. I really appreciate the lift."

No reply. The guy next to me was smoking. He kept his head turned away from me and tapped his fingers nervously on his lap. I couldn't see the two in front either. They dragged on their cigarettes and sat rigidly, staring straight ahead. The back seat was filled with empty cups, McDonald's containers, and other junk. The car smelled of cigarette smoke, stale french fries, and alcohol.

"Kinda cool out tonight, huh?" I said.

Still no reply.

Terrific, I thought. I'm trying to go to a retreat and I get picked up by three guys who've had too many beers after work and are cruising downtown on a Friday night. What if we get into an accident? What if . . .

Suddenly the driver veered off onto a darkened side street and hit the gas. We were speeding down a narrow corridor of poverty—crumbling tenements, abandoned store fronts, vacant lots filled with weeds. We were in the part of Cleveland called "the district," where murders took place in the open air, drug dealers peddled their wares to junior high kids, and children grew up amid food stamps, fights, and fear.

"Excuse me?" I ventured. "I'm going straight down Euclid, and . . ."

"Shut up, kid," the driver snapped. "Just stay cool. We'll get there."

My heart raced and sweat broke out on my head and hands. I couldn't jump out of the car; there were only two doors. I didn't think it would be a good idea to scream; I had been told to shut up. Besides, who paid any attention to screams in this part of town? We zig-zagged up and down the deserted streets, tires squalling. "Lord, help me," I prayed silently.

The car screeched to a stop at the end of a darkened alley. A couple of cats peered curiously at the car's headlights from behind some garbage cans. Otherwise there wasn't a sign of life. The driver cut the engine.

The three guys all spun toward me and jammed .32 caliber revolvers against my head. Two cold steel barrels pressed against my throbbing temples, the third against my forehead.

"Jesus . . . Jesus . . . In the name of Jesus, please let me go," I whispered.

"Get the hell out of the car, man!"

"In the name of Jesus . . . please . . ."

They grabbed my gym bag. The guy next to me cursed and pushed me out of the car. I stood paralyzed as they frisked me and took my wallet. People were robbed and murdered in alleys like this all the time, I thought. Now it's going to happen to me!

My head filled with all kinds of crazy thoughts. I'll miss graduation. I promise never to hitchhike again. I was really looking forward to the retreat.

"Start walking toward that fence, kid," the driver ordered, waving his pistol. "And don't turn around."

I'm going to be shot in the back, I thought. They're going to kill me right here in this stinking alley. They *have* to kill me. I've seen their faces; I can identify them.

The fence was about fifty feet away across a parking lot strewn with garbage. That's probably the last thing I'll see, I thought. So much I'd like to do. So much I could do for the Lord. "Jesus, Jesus," I murmured as I stumbled toward the fence. Time stretched out as I waited for the bullet to come. What would it feel like?

Just then I heard the car engine start up. I didn't dare turn around. The tires screeched. Were they going to run me down rather than shoot me? I imagined the story in the newspaper: "Unidentified man found mortally wounded . . . ."

Suddenly I realized they were gone. Everything was over. In the stillness of the night all I could hear was the chirping of crickets and the distant sound of an ambulance siren. My heart was pounding and my body was shaking as I fell to my knees in thanksgiving. My life had been spared.

My deliverance that Friday night was nothing less than miraculous. I knew that God had spared me because he had other plans for my life. I had a special destiny that had yet to be fulfilled.

You may have had an experience like mine: a close brush with death that left you feeling as though you'd been specially protected and allowed to live. Or perhaps, when you were a young child, someone told you God had created you to do something special for him. Or you may have always had an intuitive sense that God had definite plans for your future and was specially watching over you.

Don't dismiss such thoughts as foolish. They're based on the biblical reality that the living God has called you into being. He tells you: "You did not choose me, but I chose you and *appointed* you, that you should go and bear fruit" (Jn 15:16). You have a special assignment from your maker, a divine appointment that no one else can fulfill.

God has a tailor-made plan for every life. He's asking you to dare to believe in that plan, and to believe that he is "able to do immeasurably more than all we ask or imagine, according to his power that is at work within us" (Eph 3:20).

That is the basic premise of this book: that God wants to use our lives to make a difference in the world in a time of mounting challenges. He arranges circumstances—which many dismiss as mere coincidences—in order to fashion us to fulfill our unique destiny. Awareness of these "divine appointments" and active responses to them is what spells the difference between a lackluster faith and a robust Christian life.

There are two Sauls spoken of in Scripture, one in the Old

Testament and one in the New Testament. What the Bible speaks of these two towering figures is quite revealing.

> For I am already being poured out like a drink offering, and the time has come for my departure. I have fought the good fight, I have finished the race, I have kept the faith. Now there is in store for me the crown of righteousness, which the Lord, the righteous Judge, will award to me on that day—and not only to me, but also to all who have longed for his appearing. (2 Tm 4:6-8)

> Surely I have acted like a fool and have erred greatly. (1 Sm 26:21)

One is a champion's declaration—the triumphant shout of a man who took hold of his destiny in life. The other is a beaten man's lament—the tragic regret of a man whose destiny was never achieved.

God has a unique plan for each of our lives. Psalm 138:8 says, "The Lord will fulfill his purpose for me." True fulfillment comes from knowing this truth and daily co-operating with God as he brings it to fruition. Rather than investing our lives in things that don't matter and don't last, rather than growing old dreaming of what our lives could have been, we are challenged by God to seize our destiny. This is our divine appointment in the generation in which we are called to live.

How exciting to realize that from the foundation of the world God ordained you and me to be alive during this particular period of history, to make a unique contribution to his kingdom. The words of Esther apply to each of us: "Who knows whether thou art come to the kingdom for such a time as this?" (Est 4:14).

Years ago, singer Diana Ross expressed in song what I believe is still the heart-cry of multitudes in the generation around us:

Do you know where you're going to?
Do you like the things that life is showing you?
Where are you going to. . . ?
Do you know. . . ?

These haunting words raise questions that few can answer. "Why am I here? What is my purpose for living? Was I created for anything special?"

The world tells us we are a biological happenstance and that our only purpose in life is to survive and to "look out for number one."

But we know better. We know that God made us, that we are his special creation, and that he has a particular plan for our lives and for his people in this time in history. We hear God speaking to us as he spoke to Jeremiah, "Before I formed you in the womb I knew you, before you were born I set you apart; I appointed you as a prophet to the nations" (Jer 1:5). We may not all be appointed to be prophets, but we all have an appointment—an assigned task for our lives. Jesus put it this way: "He [the Son of God] leaves his house in charge of his servants, each with his assigned task, and tells the one at the door to keep watch" (Mk 13:34).

I believe that every man and woman has an assigned task, that every person's life is designed by God, that each of us has a role selected by God from all eternity. One day we shall have another divine appointment, before the judgment seat of Christ (see Rom 14:10), to give an account of how well we have fulfilled our mission. "It is *appointed* unto men once to die, but after this the judgment" (Heb 9:27). I also believe God has a plan for his people in each generation: "David . . . served God's purpose *in his own generation*" (Acts 13:36). This is our destiny, our divine appointment.

"If you would do the best with your life," British leader Arthur Wallis has said, "find out what God is doing in your generation and fling yourself into it."

As we grow in the awareness that God has had his hand on

us since before we were born, we realize more and more that events we once saw as mere coincidence, as "things just falling into place," actually have their origin in God and fit together in God's plan for our life. God orchestrates events to fashion us so that we can fulfill our unique calling.

"Many of us think, after a number of years," notes author J. Oswald Sanders, "that we are finally entering the purpose of God for our life, when actually it is the culmination of a preparatory process which began before our birth." How true; may God help us to recognize his superintending providence operating in our personal lives.

Without becoming fatalistic about it—imagining our lives as neatly pre-packaged and fast-frozen, progressively thawed out in the great microwave oven of life—are we really aware that much of what happens to us is not mere coincidence, but providence? As Frederick Meyer, one of the biographers of the apostle Paul, puts it:

> A providence is shaping our ends; a plan is developing in our lives; a supremely wise and loving Being is making all things work together for good. In the sequel of our life's story we shall see there was a meaning and necessity in all the previous incidents, save those which are the result of our own folly and sin, and that even those have been made to contribute to the final result.

As Meyer points out, God is not responsible for all the calamities of life. Much is simply the result of ignorance or disobedience to divine law. And yet how many of our significant life experiences—even the hard ones—have actually originated in the heart of God? The apostle Paul said, "No man should be moved by these afflictions; for you yourselves know that we are *appointed* to these things" (1 Thes 3:3).

Even in the case of Job, God begins by granting Satan permission to afflict him: "Very well, then, everything he has is in your hands" (Job 1:12). Job's afflictions were for him a divine appointment arranged by God.

But note that Job's ordeal was not a life sentence. It came to an end after several months, when God healed his body, provided him with a new family and twice the flocks, camels, and crops he had begun with. He even lived for 140 more years. His deliverance came when he acknowledged his difficulty as a divine appointment, broke out of his prison of self-pity, and began to serve others in their need. "After Job prayed for his friends, the Lord made him prosperous again and gave him twice as much as he had before" (Job 42:10).

Some of us see a difficulty in every opportunity. But we can learn to see an opportunity in every difficulty. Have you trained yourself to approach each day as a sacred trust in which your loving heavenly Father orchestrates the affairs of your life to make you more like himself and to use you to serve his purpose in this generation? "And we know that in all things God works for the good of those who love him, who have been called according to his purpose. For those God foreknew he also predestined to be conformed to the likeness of his Son, that he might be the firstborn among many brothers" (Rom 8:28, 29).

Have you embraced the truth that even before your birth, God had written in his book your days' events? "My frame was not hidden from you when I was made in the secret place. When I was woven together in the depths of the earth, your eyes saw my unformed body. All the days *ordained* for me were written in your book before one of them came to be. How precious to me are your thoughts, O God! How vast is the sum of them!" (Ps 139:15-17).

Even the opportunities for doing good that come to us are pre-arranged by our Father in heaven: "For we are God's workmanship, created in Christ Jesus to do good works, which God prepared in advance for us to do" (Eph 2:10).

Imagine it: God has already established good works for us and strategically placed them in our path. We don't need to search high and low for them; he brings them to us (or, rather, he brings us to them). We need only be alert to them and stir ourselves to act upon them.

Instead of waking up each day and sputtering, "Good Lord, it's morning!" we can exclaim, "Good morning, Lord! This is the day that you yourself have made for me. I'm going to rejoice and be glad in it, and make it count for you" (see Ps 118:24).

Even when we face difficulties, we can remember that "Because of the Lord's great love we are not consumed, for his compassions never fail. They are new every morning; great is your faithfulness" (Lam 3:22-23). We can confidently pray, "Lord, help me to remember that nothing is going to happen to me today that you and I together can't handle. By your grace and power, I'm an 'overcomer.' I'll come over the obstacles in my way by the power of your Spirit. 'Greater is he that is in me than he that is in the world'" (see 1 Jn 5:4; 4:4).

The time has come, amid the increasing needs of today's world, for a whole new generation of Christians to rise up and meet the divine appointment God has arranged for them. God wants to form a generation of uncompromising, valiant believers who will seize their unique destiny and give their lives away to serve God's grand purpose in our day: the restoration of authentic New Testament Christianity to reach the nations with his glorious good news. He wants to form a generation driven by a holy determination to live radical and heroic lives for him in order to get the job done!

It has been said that there are three groups of people in the world: the *few* who make things happen, the *many* who watch things happen, the *majority* who don't know what's happening.

Someone else divided the world into four groups: the *wishbones* who wish someone would do something, the *jawbones* who talk a lot but do nothing, the *knucklebones* who knock whatever anyone tries to do, and the *backbones* who get under the load, do the work, and alter the course of history.

God wants us to be among the priceless few who shake off apathy, lethargy, and defeatism, pick up their share of the load, and help God renew the face of the earth. He wants us to "lay hold of that for which Christ Jesus took hold of us" (see Phil 3:12). It would be tragic to ignore this call or to act as though it is beyond our ability to respond to what God wants to do through us.

Hetty Green provides a sobering example. She was a multimillionaire. Yet when she died in 1916, with an estate valued at over $100 million, she was known as "America's Greatest Miser." Among other eccentricities she ate cold oatmeal to avoid the expense of heating it. Her son had to have his leg amputated because she searched in vain for a free medical clinic to treat him. She even hastened her own demise by provoking an attack of apoplexy while arguing over the merits of drinking skim milk. She is a symbol of many Christians today who though blessed with abundant resources, act as though they have nothing to contribute to the kingdom.

My prayer is that *Divine Appointments* will inspire in you a new awareness of the providence, provision, and protection of God that is constantly at work, molding your life for usefulness in his kingdom in these critical hours of history. The blessings and workings of God are, moment by moment, either moving you forward or passing you by: are you alert to them?

Will you dare to believe in God's overriding care and intervention in the affairs of your life? Even amid trials, will you place unwavering confidence in his ability to navigate through them? Will you resolve to "trust in the Lord with all your heart and lean not on your own understanding; in all your ways acknowledge him, and he will make your paths straight" (Prv 3:5-6)?

Will you join me in the adventure of living each day with a sense of expectancy, "being confident of this, that he who began a good work in you will carry it on to completion until the day of Christ Jesus" (Phil 1:6)?

Will you decide to take hold of your destiny, to keep the divine appointment God has arranged for you, to cooperate with his Spirit in making each day of your life a masterpiece for God? Will you, like David, serve the purpose of God in your generation and join with scores of Christians around the world to see the church restored in purity, in power, and in patterns of holy living, to reach our world for Jesus Christ?

TWO

More than Conquerors

O NE EVENING MY WIFE AND I took our four children out for dinner at a local pizzeria, one that featured a room filled with all kinds of video games and other electronic gadgets. We bought some tokens and turned the kids loose.

One game consisted of a large level surface with six holes in it. Every so often a "ground hog" would pop his head up through one of the holes, as the player tried to bop him with a large mallet.

This game became a particular favorite of my six-year-old son Justin. He stood there, eyes fixed on the game board, mallet at the ready, just waiting to slam the poor little creature on the head and drive him back down into his hole.

Many of us approach life in a way that reminds me of that game. Every time we try to rise up, walk victoriously, and seize our destiny in life, something inside us says, "Oh, no you don't!" and pounds us over the head with the mallet of defeatism. "You're no good," we tell ourselves. "You're a failure. You'll never amount to anything."

Where does that "something" inside us come from? Maybe it stems from our past: we've been told by our parents or our teachers that we will "never amount to anything," and we have believed it. Maybe it comes from a poor self-image stemming from genuine personal problems. Maybe it is rooted in fear: we have experienced failure before and would rather not risk it again. Maybe our enemy, the devil, is whispering lies in our ear and we are listening to him. "The Spirit of the Lord is upon me . . . to *appoint* unto those who mourn in Zion, to give unto them beauty for ashes, the oil of joy for mourning, the garment of praise for the spirit of heaviness, that they might be called trees of righteousness, the planting of the Lord, that he might be glorified" (Is 61:1-3; KJV). Wherever our negative, defeatist attitude comes from, God wants to help us get rid of it. Rather than struggling with a low self-image, wandering aimlessly through life, "mourning in Zion," he gives us "beauty for ashes" through a new identity in him. He gives us security and identity, like "trees of righteousness, the planting of the Lord." He provides us with a definite sense of purpose and direction in life. Our responsibility is to believe him, and to give ourselves away in serving him.

Not that God is blind to various weaknesses, failings, and limitations. "For he knows our frame; he remembers that we are dust" (Ps 103:14). No, God understands full well what he has to work with when he decides to work with you and me. But the Bible makes clear that God has a long history of doing extraordinary things through ordinary people, raising them above themselves by the power of his Spirit as they give themselves over to him.

When the people of Israel were preparing to take possession of the promised land, Joshua led a scouting party of twelve men to spy out the terrain. Two of the men, Joshua and Caleb, came back from the scouting expedition full of faith and readiness to take the land. "It's fabulous! Just like God said it would be. Milk and honey and grapes *this big* . . . Sure, there were some enemy soldiers and fortified cities, but nothing we can't handle with God's help." But the others told quite a different tale. "We can't attack those people; they're stronger than we are . . . the land we explored devours those living in it. All the people we saw there are of great size. . . . We seemed like grasshoppers in our own eyes, and we looked the same to them" (see Nm 13:27-28, 31-33).

Twelve men went to explore the land. All twelve saw the same things—including the "giants" and the fortified cities. But only Caleb and Joshua saw them through God's eyes. Not only that, but Caleb and Joshua saw *themselves* through God's eyes, as strong warriors able to conquer the obstacles before them by the power of his Spirit. They were men of "a different spirit." The others saw themselves through the lens of their own inadequacies: "We seemed like grasshoppers *in our own eyes.*" Their image of themselves made them draw back from the divine appointment God had given them.

How many of us, when we consider the challenges that confront us in pursuing our destiny in life and in seeing the church become what God wants it to be, make the same mistake? We see ourselves and our capabilities, not with eyes of faith but only in terms of our weaknesses and limitations. "Look at me. Look at the shape the world is in. Look at the condition of the church. It's no use."

The real problem isn't with the obstacles that confront us from without, or even with the human weaknesses that limit us from within. The real problem is that we fall back into defeatism and fail to trust God to work *through* us, individually and corporately, in achieving his purposes. We never even give God a chance to "show himself strong" on our behalf (see 2 Chr 16:9).

I could easily have fallen into this pattern myself. In human terms, my upbringing offered plenty of excuses for a half-hearted approach to life. My father, who had come to America from Poland as a boy, never finished high school and went through life losing one job after another. My mother worked as a scrubwoman to help make ends meet, despite a painful physical disability. They never owned a car. They were both just shy of forty when their children were born. What kind of destiny might seem to await a young man from that kind of background?

But when I committed my life to Jesus Christ, I realized

from the outset that I needed to reject any self-imposed limits on what he could do with me. God had a plan for my life and for his people in this hour of destiny. Then as now, he was looking for ordinary people—like me—to use in an extra-ordinary way. My job was simply to trust and obey, give myself over to God's purpose, and let him unfold his plan. The words I have carried in my wallet for over a decade became my motto—"The world has not yet seen what God will do with and in and through the man whose life is wholly consecrated to him."

In the years since then I've been privileged to travel throughout the United States and around the world, challenging people to commit their lives totally to Jesus Christ, to get planted in a church embodying authentic New Testament Christianity, and to join in the unparalleled adventure of pursuing the exciting purposes of God in our generation. God has permitted me to be used in awakening people to their divine destiny; to serve as student president of a 14,000 member university; to preach at conferences and miracle services in the U.S. and abroad; to launch an international magazine, *People of Destiny*; to appear on numerous television programs; to speak to professional football teams; and to lead an apostolic team involved in planting churches throughout the country. I get none of the credit, for all of it has only been possible in and through him. I've simply chosen not to "limit the Holy One of Israel" (God's chosen people's primary sin) and to dare to believe my life could make a difference. Whatever your weaknesses, whatever limitations your background or upbringing seems to impose on you, whatever trials and obstacles you now face, you too can be used by God to influence scores of people through your life.

It hasn't all been glory, however. God has led me through many struggles during these years, to mold and shape me for maximum usefulness. I've faced physical infirmities, a multi-million dollar lawsuit, and other challenges too numerous to mention. At times I have been tempted to quit. Yet his grace has always sustained me. As I have called out to him in faith, he has given me the strength to press on to victory. I have discovered that if you can stand the pull, Jesus will always pull you through!

Man's strategy is to change the world through power, money, intelligence, influence. God's strategy is to change the world through the efforts of seemingly insignificant people. He took a nation of despised Hebrew slaves and ushered in a new society. He chose a puny shepherd boy named David to slay the fearsome giant, Goliath. He sent his Son to be born in a stable in order to redeem mankind. He assembled twelve uneducated and unsophisticated men to establish his church.

"Think of what *you* were when you were called," Paul writes. "Not many of you were wise by human standards; not many were influential; not many were of noble birth. But God chose the foolish things of the world to shame the wise; God chose the weak things of the world to shame the strong. He chose the lowly things of this world and the despised things—and the things that are not—to nullify the things that are, so that no one may boast before him" (1 Cor 1:26-29).

In other words, God chooses in an upside down manner! He says, "I know some in my kingdom appear rich and mighty but 'not many.'" And many today who appear dynamic and mighty didn't come in that way. Those who were that way in the beginning—like Moses and Paul—have gone through a sifting and sorting that few would envy. So if you feel foolish, weak, lowly, or despised—take heart. You're in the majority! God declares, *The thing that you think disqualifies you actually qualifies you!*

God is not looking for self-sufficient people, people who seem to have their lives in perfect order. He's looking for men and women who are willing to be obedient and to place their trust in a limitless God. God loves to take people who seem like flops, fill them with resurrection life and power, and use them to turn the world upside down.

We need to discard our puny vision for our own lives and for the church and begin to see ourselves as God sees us. We are world-changers, godly heroes, champions of righteousness. We are called to do "exploits" of faith and to exert a powerful influence for the kingdom of God. The church is not to be impotent, viewed as irrelevant by society. It is to be "the joy of the whole earth" (see Ps 48:2), an alternative society, a counterculture, God's instrument to impact the watching world.

Don't let negative thinking, shyness, or self-consciousness dominate your life. Don't set your sights too low and prevent God from leading you into your destiny. Inside of you are miracles waiting to be released, ideas waiting to be expressed, songs and books that may be waiting to be written, ideas waiting to be expressed. You are called to become a part of God's end-time move to restore his church and alter the course of history. Don't settle for mediocrity, for drifting along in a life of meaningless personal pleasure. As the people of God, we are destined for greatness in these climactic hours of human history.

The time has come for us to recognize that we are in a spiritual conflict with the forces of darkness who want to lie to us about who we are and what we can become in Christ, who want us to believe the lie that the church cannot fulfill its destiny. We need to rise up, reject the discouraging words of the evil one, and seize our destiny in God. If God is who he says he is, and *we* are who he says we are, then we can do the things he says we can!

A seventeen-year-old girl sustained a devastating injury that left her paralyzed from the neck down. But, having placed her life in the hands of a limitless God, she refused to resign herself to a life of self-pity and unfruitfulness. In the years since her tragic accident, Joni Eareckson Tada has written two books that have been published in almost forty languages world-wide, recorded two albums, starred in a film version of her own life story, and produced a stream of artwork (paintings, pen-and-ink drawings, and sketches) that astound many able-bodied artists. She is unable to use her arms and legs, but God is able to use her mightily.

As a youngster, another woman suffered from an eye infection. A doctor mistakenly prescribed medicine that caused her to lose her sight completely. But instead of giving up, she trusted God to bring her many gifts to fruition. In time she composed songs and hymns that became popular throughout the world and remain in use to this day. The next time you sing "To God Be the Glory" or "Blessed Assurance," remember this remarkable woman of God: Fanny Crosby.

A few years ago a young boy struggled through school, apparently academically handicapped. It took him two years to pass first grade, and then only on probation. In fact, five different times during his grade school years he passed only on probation. It was in high school that a friend challenged him to the discipline of Scripture meditation and memorization. That became the pad from which God launched him into a youth ministry renowned the world over for its insight and pastoral astuteness. Perhaps you or someone you know has attended the Institute in Basic Youth Conflicts taught by Bill Gothard.

John Geddie was another man with an overcomer's attitude. As a missionary, he spent twenty-four years evangelizing the people in the remote corner of the world to which God had called him. His tombstone reads, "When he landed in 1848 there were no Christians. When he left in 1872 there were no heathen."

A father found that his children had trouble following the old-fashioned language of the King James Bible during their family devotions. But whenever he re-phrased the Scriptures in his own words, the youngsters followed along avidly. An idea came to him: "Why not paraphrase the entire Bible?"

Though he had no commitment from any publisher, he decided to undertake the massive project.

Already in his forties, he spent more than sixteen years laboring over every book, chapter, verse, and word to make the Bible more readily understandable to the average reader. His intense concern that he be scrupulously faithful to the meaning of God's word placed him under such tremendous stress that his vocal chords began to deteriorate and he was barely able to speak for almost fifteen years.

Then, when at long last he completed this monumental task, he could find no one willing to publish the manuscript. He was rejected by five different publishers. His years of grueling work seemed wasted.

But he refused to give up on what he still felt certain was an assigned task from the Lord. He decided to publish the manuscript himself. He ran off two thousand copies and promised all the royalties to the Lord. That was the beginning of Tyndale House, now a major Christian publisher. Today, copies of Ken Taylor's *Living Bible* number not two thousand, but more than twenty million. Perhaps you've seen it recently re-released under the title *The Book*.

A young man named William Carey, nicknamed "the foolish shoemaker" by his critics, once attended a minister's conference where the complacency was so thick you could cut it with a knife. When he asked "whether or not the Great Commission is binding on us today to go and teach all nations," an older minister rebuked him. "Sit down, young man," the minister fumed. "When God pleases to convert the heathen, he'll well do it without your aid or mine."

After much prayer, William obeyed the Holy Spirit and went to India. He evangelized millions. He translated the Bible into four of the leading languages. He mobilized others to translate it into thirty-two other Asian languages. He also established 126 Christian mission schools and an Indian mission college. His motto? "Attempt great things for God. Expect great things from God!"

Years ago a black man in the South, quite familiar with the racial prejudice that could have destroyed him, surrendered his life to Christ and claimed as his life verse Philippians 4:13: "I can do all things through Christ who strengthens me." Trained as a scientist, one day he went into a laboratory and said, "Dear Mr. Creator, please tell me what the universe was made for." He sensed an impression in his spirit, "That's too much for your little mind. Ask for something more your size." So he asked, "Mr. Creator, please tell me what man was made for." Again he sensed, "Little man, you are still asking too much." Finally he asked, "Well, Mr. Creator, will you tell me why the peanut was made?"

In time this man, who could have been overwhelmed by his circumstances, invented 300 uses for the peanut, 118 uses for the sweet potato and 75 uses for the pecan. His work revolutionized the South, transforming it from dependence on cotton farming, which was robbing the soil of nutrients, to peanut farming, which built the soil back up.

Next time you or your children spread a little peanut butter, remember this inventor—a godly Christian, George Washington Carver.

In 1898, two Christian men traveling through Wisconsin chanced to meet in a hotel and decided to have evening devotions together. They appreciated this rare opportunity for Christian fellowship while traveling and expressed the wish that it could happen more often. Before long they were discussing the idea of forming some kind of association for Christian travelers.

A few months later they got together again, along with a third man. By now their wistful idea had taken a more definite shape, and the scope of their thinking had greatly expanded. "How," they asked, "might we spread the gospel and win converts among the many people traveling away from home?"

These were the days before mass media, mass production, mass communication, and mass transportation. The group numbered only three, with few resources at their command. The task before them was enormous. But so was their conviction that the God who had called them to it would see them through it. They decided to step out in faith, taking the name of a Bible character who, under God's direction, had led a tiny band against a great army and emerged victorious.

Today, the ministry they founded reaches into almost every hotel and motel room in the civilized world. The last time you stayed overnight in a motel, you may have paused for a few moments' meditation with a Bible provided by the Gideons.

These are but a few examples of what can happen when ordinary men and women, energized by the Spirit of God, decide to cast off negativity and self-doubt and act like the conquerors God has made them to be.

As George Fox, founder of the Quakers, put it: "One man raised by God's power to stand and live in the same spirit as the apostles and prophets can shake the country for ten miles around."

John Wesley, founder of Methodism, put it this way: "Give me one hundred men who love only God with all their heart, and hate only sin with all their heart, and we will shake the gates of hell and bring in the kingdom of God in one generation." It was Wesley who told his followers, "When you go out to preach, don't worry about how to gain an audience. Get on fire, and people will come to watch you burn!"

No discussion of rising above our limitations—whether self-imposed or imposed by outside factors—would be complete without considering the unique challenges confronting Christian women today.

Many women—especially mothers with small children, battle with a low self-image that holds them back from taking hold of their destiny. The media stereotypes the woman who stays at home as slow-witted, frumpy, and unfulfilled (in contrast, of course, to the female career executive who is beautiful, intelligent, impeccably dressed, and perfectly self-actualized). You have seen her in dozens of television commercials: slumped over the washing machine, grief-stricken by ring-around-the-collar; staring dumbly at her bathroom sink as disembodied Drano voices criticize her substandard housekeeping.

These are humorous examples. But millions of women have been brainwashed into seeing themselves through society's distorted lens. Self-respect among women is at an all-time low. "If I could write a prescription for the women of the world," says noted family authority Dr. James Dobson, "I would provide each one of them with a healthy dose of self-esteem and personal worth (taken four times a day, until the symptoms disappear). I have no doubt this is their greatest need."

If you find yourself nodding and saying, "That's me, all right," God wants to help you recapture a vision for the importance and dignity of being a mother and for the important part you have to play in the restoration of the church and the evangelization of the world. He wants to help you resist societal pressures and embrace the high calling of motherhood. He wants you to stop putting youself down and apologizing for yourself because of your state in life.

In her excellent book, *Marriage to a Difficult Man,* Elizabeth Dodds illustrates how a mother's contribution continues to impact the world for generations after her. She studies the descendants of Sarah Edwards, wife of famous eighteenth-century preacher Jonathan Edwards and mother of eleven, and chronicles the achievements and contributions of those children and their offspring. Out of 1,400 Edwards descendants, the family produced:

- 13 college presidents
- 65 professors
- 100 lawyers and a dean of a law school
- 30 judges
- 66 physicians and a dean of a medical school

-80 public office holders, including
3 mayors
3 governors
3 United States senators
a controller of the United States treasury
a vice-president of the United States.

Was Sarah Edwards able to foresee all this as she cared for her children and invested her love and values in them through the everyday routine of life? With her natural eyes, no. But with the eyes of faith . . . .

It was Abraham Lincoln, whose mother died when he was only ten, who said, "All that I am and all that I shall be I owe to my mother." If you are a mother pressured by today's prejudice against motherhood, capture this vision and make it your own. You don't need to desert your loved ones and your station in life in order to fulfill your divine appointment. You are living it *now*. Celebrate it for all it's worth! Give your life away in service to your husband, to your children, to other Christians, to evangelizing the lost, and see what fulfillment you will derive!

Whatever your calling in life, don't let your weaknesses and limitations—real or imagined, internally or externally imposed—rob you of your destiny. "The eyes of the Lord run to and fro throughout the whole earth in order to show himself strong on behalf of those whose hearts are blameless towards him" (2 Chr 16:9). What about you? Isn't it time you rise up in faith and obedience, throw off the fetters of your own unbelief and apparent inadequacies, and take hold of the destiny God has prepared for you as he sets about restoring his church?

THREE

Seizing Your Destiny

G OD HAS A UNIQUE CALL and purpose for each of our lives. He wants us to break out of mediocrity, out of a dull and aimless existence, in order to step into a life of purpose and vision, fulfilling the assigned task he has set before us. He wants us to play a part in the restoration of his church so he can effectively reach this world with the gospel of Jesus Christ.

Well and good, you say. But how do we go about it? What can we actually *do,* in concrete, practical terms, that will help us keep our divine appointment with destiny? In this chapter I offer ten simple, practical steps that you can begin taking right now. Each one is a giant step toward taking hold of your destiny in God.

Be Certain You Are a Christian and Committed in a Church of Genuine Biblical Faith

I cannot emphasize strongly enough that our destiny lies totally in the hands of the living God and that its fulfillment depends entirely on the grace of God mediated through his Son, Jesus Christ. It is God who has brought us into being, who "knitted us together in our mother's womb" (see Ps 139:13) according to a definite plan and purpose that is his and his alone. It is he who controls the times and seasons of our lives, arranging circumstances, orchestrating events, guiding our steps according to his will. Apart from him, our life has no ultimate meaning. It is he in whom we live and move and have our being.

Moreover, it is only in and through Jesus Christ that we can be incorporated into God's purposes and integrated into his master plan. The Bible teaches that in and of ourselves we are sinful, cut off from God by our own stubbornness and disobedience. No effort of our own, however sincerely motivated or ardently pursued, can bring us back into that deep union with God which we forfeited by our sin. Only the atoning death of Jesus Christ, only his blood shed on the cross, can bridge the spiritual chasm that separates mankind from God and restores us to fellowship with him.

Thus the indispensable first step toward taking hold of your destiny is to make certain that you are, indeed, a Christian and involved in a church which expresses authentic New Testament Christianity. Many people assume they are Christian because they "live in a Christian area" or because their parents were Christians, or because they "try to be a good person and do good to others," or even because they go to church on Sunday.

But none of these is sufficient. It is only as each of us, individually, accepts Christ's finished work on the cross, surrenders his life to Christ's lordship by repentance and faith, and commits himself to radical obedience to God's will, that we are born anew into the family of God, launched into the "abundant life" (Jn 10:10), and made absolutely certain about our entrance into heaven upon our death. If you have never made a definite, clear-cut decision to give your life to Jesus Christ, I urge you to do it right now by praying this simple prayer:

Lord Jesus Christ, I want to belong to you from now on. I admit I cannot save myself by any "good works" I may do. I want to be freed from the dominion of darkness and the rule of Satan, and I want to enter into your kingdom and be part of your people. I will turn away from all wrong-doing, and I will, empowered by your Spirit, avoid anything that is opposed to your will. I repent for the sins I have committed and ask you to forgive me for them. I now put all my trust in you, and you alone, for my salvation. I offer my life to you, and I promise to obey you and serve you totally as my Lord. I freely receive your gift of eternal life and ask you to release the power of your Holy Spirit in my life to make me fruitful as your servant.

As you begin your new life in Christ, make it a habit to spend time with the Lord each day in prayer and Scripture meditation. Pray that God will lead you to a church that expresses authentic New Testament Christianity, where you can serve others, be nurtured in your faith, receive encouragement and correction, and be trained to fulfill the role God has for you. Above all, trust that the Lord has his hand upon your life and has an exciting adventure awaiting you as he moves by his Spirit to restore his glorious church.

Appreciate Your Unconditional Acceptance by God

Each of us, all day every day, is fed a steady diet of lies about what it means to be an acceptable person. Our culture, especially through the media, bombards us continually with subtle, and not-so-subtle, messages that tear down our self-esteem. "You've got to be cool to be accepted." "You've got to produce." "You've got to measure up." "You've got to use this product to be a real man (or woman)." "Your skin is aging and your teeth are dingy. You don't wear the right clothes, have the right car, or use the right cologne. You're not thin enough, either, and your hair is drab."

The situation is compounded by the fact that our enemy, Satan, uses accusations as his number one weapon against us (see Rv 12:10). He wants us to feel unworthy as individuals, and especially as Christians. "Who are you trying to kid? You call yourself a Christian? You really expect God to forgive you, after all you've done?"

Faulty religious training can cause us to slip into a performance-based, legalistic approach to gaining God's favor. "If I just witness to ten more people . . . . If I just get up an hour earlier to pray . . . . If I can just read through the Bible in a month . . . *then* God will love me." But sooner or later we slip and fall under condemnation.

God wants to free us from the lies of our culture and from the slanders of Satan. He wants to shatter worldly counterfeits and the bondage of legalism and to empower us to rise above Satan's fiery darts. He wants us to lay hold of this simple but revolutionary truth: that he loves us and accepts us, not because of what we do or don't do but because of who we are—his children, saved by his grace, forgiven by his mercy, adopted into his family, being transformed into the image and likeness of his Son Jesus Christ.

"Accept one another, then, just as Christ accepted you" (Rom 15:7). If we haven't grasped by revelation our unconditional acceptance by God, it will adversely affect the way we relate to others. We will communicate rejection and conditional love, which will hinder our personal growth and development.

"But how could God love me?" you ask. "I'm not good enough. I don't deserve it."

Ah, but that is precisely the point. He doesn't love you because you are good; you are good because he loves you! And you don't have to earn his love; you only have to accept it by faith.

If you have been jilted, if you feel ugly, if you struggle with your parents, if you are overweight or underweight, if you have been divorced, if you have lost your job, if you're consumed by remorse over past sexual involvements—God loves you anyway. He may not approve of all you have done or do, but he accepts and loves you. Receive his love. It will change your life! Shake off self-pity and take hold of the promise of Scripture: "If God is for us, who can be against us?" (Rom 8:31).

Celebrate Your God-given Value and Uniqueness

How often have you heard others—or maybe yourself—say things like: "I'm too short . . . too tall . . . too shy . . . too young . . . too old . . . . It's my parents . . . my lack of education . . . my physical deficiencies . . . I'm living in the wrong place . . ."?

We are constantly underselling ourselves because of imagined or self-imposed limitations. Sometimes we even blame God for our supposed shortcomings. "Why did you make me like this, God? Is this really the best you could do?"

God has a sobering word for us on that score. "Woe to him who quarrels with his Maker . . . . Does the clay say to the potter, 'What are you making?'. . . Do you question me about my children, or give me orders about the work of my hands?" (Is 45:9, 11). The Lord is the master potter, and we are the clay, molded and formed by him exactly the way he wants us to be.

"We are God's workmanship," Paul declares (see Eph 2:10). The original language of Scripture implies that "we are *continually* his workmanship"—not a finished product but a magnificent work in progress. The word translated "workmanship" carries the sense of "creative masterpiece." Did you realize that you are a masterpiece of the God of heaven?

We sometimes measure value by how much something costs. By that measure our value is incalculable. We were "bought at a price," Scripture tells us (1 Cor 6:20). And what a price! It was paid not in gold or silver or precious gems but in the blood of God's own Son. It was the ultimate price, and God gladly paid it for every one of us.

When I was in grade school science class, I was amazed to learn that no two snowflakes are identical. Think of it: with the countless billions of snowflakes that have ever fallen, God has taken the trouble to see that no two are ever the same. He has taken no less trouble with us. When he made each one of us, he gave us a set of fingerprints and threw away the mold. That, of course, is only a token of the uniqueness we have as fully formed human beings.

There is nobody else exactly like you; never has been, never will be. You are a once-in-an-eternity, never-to-be-repeated, special creation of God.

Embrace Discipline

In my Bible I have written the words, "Go for it!" above a passage that has inspired me for years: "Do you not know that in a race all the runners run, but only one gets the prize? Run in such a way as to get the prize. Everyone who competes in the games goes into strict training. They do it to get a crown that will not last; but we do it to get a crown that will last forever. Therefore I do not run like a man running aimlessly; I do not fight like a man beating the air. No, I beat my body and make it my slave so that after I have preached to others, I myself will not be disqualified for the prize" (1 Cor 9:24-27).

The Greek word for "competes" is *agonizomai*, from which we get our word "agonize." It calls to mind the kind of training and discipline a champion athlete goes through in preparation for the Olympics. The point of the passage is that we must likewise embrace discipline in our spiritual life—learning to regulate our conduct by principle rather than by impulse. Of course, by discipline I do not mean mere self-effort or willpower but rather the act of humbling ourselves to admit our inadequacy and to receive God's grace so that we can go forward in "the strength of his might."

The passage also says, "Run in such a way as to get the prize," and points out that in an athletic competition there is only one prize and, therefore, only one winner. In our case, the emphasis is not so much on the singularity of the prize but on the attitude of the competitor. Launch out, not half-heartedly or with a loser's mentality but as a winner, determined to please the Lord and accomplish God-given tasks for his glory.

If God has called you to do something and other godly leaders who know you personally have confirmed it (which I believe is the scriptural approach to be followed), then humble yourself, draw upon the grace of God, and see yourself as God sees you: a winner, a champion, "more than a conqueror through Christ who loves you" (see Rom 8:37).

Break Out of the Routine

God is a God of newness. Scripture speaks of the new covenant, of new wine, of a new and living way, of a new song, of having a new name, and so on. "Forget the former things," God tells us through the prophet Isaiah, "do not dwell on the past. See, I am doing a new thing!" (Is 43:18-19).

What about you? If you are going to rise above mediocrity and be used by God, you must not be content to drift through life on the river of routine.

Do you sit in the same seat during your worship service each Sunday? Do you drive the same route to and from school or work every day? Do you eat the same cereal for breakfast every morning? Do you associate only with the same people year after year?

There's nothing wrong with developing routine approaches to things; it saves us the trouble of having to figure everything out fresh at every turn. But helpful routine can turn into staleness and deaden us to the promptings of God's Spirit as he tries to lead us in new directions. One of the ways we can open ourselves to the new things God wants to do in our lives is to embrace new challenges and to resist the tendency to get comfortable and complacent in life.

For a start, ask God to instill in you a pioneering spirit. Then look for opportunities to get "out of the rut" you may have inadvertently slipped into.

By books, tapes, or conferences, expose yourself to the exciting things God is doing in the world today. Resist sitting in the same seat all the time or traveling the same familiar path. Reach out in love to some new people. Pray and then involve yourself in a sphere of service you have thought about but never done. Rather than ordering "the usual" for lunch, try something you have never eaten before. Doing new and different things—or even doing familiar things in a new and different way—can give fresh perspective and help you cultivate a more adventurous and flexible way of life. Wait on God and then open your eyes to the vast world of opportunity surrounding you.

Learn How to Fail

It may be obvious that if we are going to try new things, we are occasionally going to experience failure. "The righteous man falls seven times," the Scriptures promise us, "yet he rises again" (Prv 24:16). I am convinced that God is more pleased with those who step out and fail than with those who sit back and do nothing out of fear of failure. God can vindicate our mistakes and bring good out of our failure. The ability to handle failure in a positive, productive way is crucial if we are to make progress in pursuing our divine appointment. Remember the stories of Peter, David, Moses, and other heroes of our Christian faith. They had enough faith to risk failure.

Charles Lindbergh, the first man to fly solo across the Atlantic, said, "What kind of man would live where there is no daring? I don't believe in taking foolish chances, but nothing can be accomplished if we won't take any chances at all."

Don't waste time brooding over yesterday's mistakes. Sure, it's okay to look back long enough to glean a lesson from a mistake. But there is no need to build a monument to it. When you are driving a car, you have to glance in the rearview mirror occasionally. But if you keep your eyes there instead of on the road in front of you, you will inevitably collide with something.

Don't let failure make you fearful of trying again. Turn your trials into triumphs, your stumbling blocks into stepping-stones, your tests into testimonies. Follow Paul's example: "Forgetting what is behind and straining toward what is ahead, I press on toward the goal to win the prize for which God has called me heavenward in Christ Jesus. All of us who are mature should take such a view of things" (Phil 3:13-15).

Anytime you are tempted to become discouraged by setbacks in life, remember the following "highlights" of Abraham Lincoln's career:

1831—Failed in business
1832—Defeated for legislature
1833—Again failed in business
1835—Sweetheart died
1836—Suffered nervous breakdown
1838—Defeated for Speaker
1840—Defeated for Elector
1843—Defeated for Congress
1848—Again defeated for Congress
1855—Defeated for Senate
1856—Defeated for Vice-President
1858—Again defeated for Senate
1860—Elected President of the United States

Even if you have been on a losing streak lately, don't lose heart. Babe Ruth is renowned for his home runs, but he also struck out more times than anyone else in baseball history. Ted Williams was baseball's greatest hitter, and even he failed six out of every ten times he went to the plate. Remember, it is during the dry seasons that roots go down deeper, preparing the way for greater growth in the future. "'For I know the plans I have for you,' declares the Lord, 'plans to prosper you and not to harm you, plans to give you hope and a future'" (Jer 29:11).

Draw Inspiration from Challenging People

"Iron sharpens iron," Scripture teaches, "and one man sharpens another" (Prv 27:17). And again, "He who walks with wise men becomes wise" (Prv 13:20). Putting ourselves in touch with wise, stimulating, faith-building people will help us move ahead in our own Christian life.

We can draw inspiration by reading about the actions of great men and women of faith. The Bible, of course, is filled with such stories. I suspect the apostles were as inspired to read the exploits of Elijah, David, and Gideon as we are. And in turn, the apostles inspire us. We can also benefit from reading the biographies of prominent Christians throughout church history. I know how much inspiration I have drawn from reading about John Wesley, Billy Graham, and others. We can also derive blessing and motivation by listening to inspiring speakers, whether in person, on tape, or via radio and television. One of the reasons we began publishing *People of Destiny* magazine was to motivate hungry Christians to fulfill their destiny in God.

Some of the people who can inspire us most are those zealous Christians in our sphere of life whose examples in character, not personality, we are to emulate. We need to make it a point to follow their example in Christ so that their faith and zeal can "rub off" on us. Scripture warns us that "bad company corrupts good morals," so we must carefully choose the company we keep. Fortunately, this principle also works the other way around: good company strengthens us in our walk with the Lord.

Discover, Develop, and Deploy Your Spiritual Gifts and God-given Talents

The value of your life as a Christian will be determined by the degree to which you use what God has given you. Stated differently: "What you are is God's gift to you. What you make of yourself is your gift back to God."

Remember the parable about the distribution of talents? The two servants who developed their talents were commended and given more. The one who let his lie dormant was severely rebuked and eventually lost what he had (see Lk 19:11-27).

Similarly, God invests in all of us certain gifts and abilities. Without exception, each of us has special gifts to be employed for others (1 Pt 4:10) and to bring glory to God. Some of the nineteen gifts listed in Scripture include teaching, leading, serving, showing mercy, giving, administration, moving in supernatural realms of faith, healing, giving a word of God-given knowledge, wisdom, and prophecy. Fulfillment in our Christian life comes as we learn that we have these gifts, identify what God has entrusted, and then step out to exercise them "for the common good."

How are we to discover our unique God-given gifts? Of course the first step is to seek God for his will. But we also need the confirmation and assistance of others in exercising the gifts. This is why we need to be a vital part of a body of Christians who believe in, teach on, and give opportunities for meaningful development and expression of the spiritual gifts.

Moreover, though we know that intellectual or academic achievement is not the same as holiness, we also know that God gave us our intelligence as a powerful tool to be used in his service. As good stewards, it is right for us to keep our minds sharp and alert, able to process new information and make decisions and form value judgments crisply and clearly. Maintaining a program of inspirational and devotional reading is one way to do this. Another is to enhance our abilities in evangelizing, child-rearing, counseling, and other areas through seminars, conferences, and tapes.

Interestingly enough, one thing that brings many people

a greater self-confidence is learning how to speak in front of an audience. You don't need to become an electrifying orator, but learning to express your ideas and speak on your feet can be a tremendous boost to your self-confidence. How are we going to preach the gospel to all nations if we can't explain it to our next-door neighbor or make a simple presentation to our class? Nervousness is natural. But we can overcome it with practice and with faith in the enabling power of God.

Give Yourself to Others and to God's Purpose in Our Generation

We must be careful not to focus so intently on "what *I* can do to pursue *my* unique calling in life" that we forget that the whole point of the Christian life is serving others. We live in a selfish, materialistic culture which emphasizes the importance of "looking out for number one." But Jesus declared, "It is more blessed to give than receive" (Acts 20:35). He also said, "A man's life does not consist in the abundance of his possessions" (Lk 12:15).

John D. Rockefeller, Sr., drove himself hard to be a success. He became a millionaire by age twenty-three and in twenty years was the richest man on earth.

One night as he struggled to fall asleep, he came to his senses as he realized his "house of cards" was tumbling down around him. He realized that he could take nothing with him beyond the grave.

The next day he embarked on a new way of living. Rather than hoarding money and possessions, he began to give them away to those in need. Establishing the Rockefeller Foundation, he channeled his fortune into hospitals, research and mission work, and gave away a portion of his riches to scores. His contributions eventually led to the discovery of penicillin. Cures for malaria, tuberculosis, and diphtheria also resulted from his giving.

At the age of fifty-three, John D. Rockefeller seemed destined for imminent death. The resolution to "give rather than get" altered his life so dramatically that he eventually lived to the ripe old age of ninety-eight!

Jesus put it this way: "Give, and it will be given to you" (Lk 6:38).

I have a plaque in my office that serves as a constant reminder of the importance of giving myself to others: "I shall pass through this world but once. Any good, therefore, that I can do, or any kindness that I can show to another human being, let me do it now. Let me not defer or neglect it, for I shall not pass this way again."

Over my fifteen years as a Christian, I have tried to apply these words, which I believe to be consistent with the words of our Lord. As I have given myself wholeheartedly in service to the purpose of God in my generation—preaching the gospel of the kingdom and fostering the restoration and revival of his church—I have found that my own life has been enriched a hundredfold.

Move Forward One Step at a Time

God tells us in his word not to "despise the day of small beginnings" (Zec 4:10). Many times people set goals that are unrealistically ambitious, and their enthusiasm quickly fades. An old saying goes, "How do you eat an elephant? One bite at a time." As you seek the Lord concerning some of the challenges that lie before you, remember to move forward one step at a time. As you make steady progress, your confidence will be bolstered and you will be able to pick up the pace. Ask the Holy Spirit to help you set appropriate goals and then to help you meet them.

An old story tells of a young boy who thought he had found a way to trick the village wise man. He caught a bird and held it in his cupped hands. Then he asked the wise man, "Is the bird alive or dead?" The old man realized that if he answered, "It is alive," the boy would crush the bird between his hands and kill it; and that if he answered, "It is dead," the boy would simply open his hands and let the bird fly away. So he looked the young man in the face and said, "My son, the answer to that question is in your hands."

As we seek to fulfill our divine appointment in life, we too need to recognize the extent of what God has placed in our hands. He has given us his Holy Spirit, his word, his call, his power. He says to us this day, "I have set before you this day life and death, blessings and curses. Now choose life" (Dt 30:19). "He is at work in us for his good pleasure," and he challenges us today by saying, "In your hands you hold the seeds of failure or the potential for greatness." It is my conviction that in this hour of church restoration to reach a lost and hurting world, we can rise up and claim our divine appointment and so fulfill our unique destiny as the people of God.

How about it? Will you "go for it"?

Part II

The Journey Continues with Divine Appointments

And of this gospel I was appointed a herald. (2 Tm 1:11)

FOUR

Always Prepared

Not long ago, my family and I spent several weeks in the Los Angeles area, planting another New Testament church. At one point during our visit, a friend and I took an afternoon off to drive around Beverly Hills and get a glimpse of how the "beautiful people" live.

As we came around a corner, we saw in front of us the famous Beverly Hills Hotel. It seemed to me like a good place to get out and take a stroll. "Who knows?" I said to my friend Steve. "Maybe God will give us an opportunity to witness to somebody famous."

Steve's initial response was less than enthusiastic. "I don't know, Larry," he said, furtively surveying the neatly manicured lawn, chauffered limousines, and opulent architecture. "Are you sure you want to do this? They might not like us poking around. Shouldn't we be heading back?"

"Aw, c'mon Steve," I chided him. "Let's see if God has anything up his sleeve!"

We made our way around to the back of the hotel. A high, ivy-covered wall separated a group of tennis courts from the rest of the grounds. We could hear the rhythmic "thwock, thwock, thwock" of a tennis ball and the squeaking of tennis shoes.

"Let's see how the game's going," I called to Steve as I

approached a small observation window in the ivy wall. What I saw inside made my jaw drop.

"St—eve!" I stammered. "Look! That guy playing tennis! It's Moses!"

"It's *who?*" said Steve, elbowing his way to the window to see for himself.

"See? Right over there! The guy who played Moses in *The Ten Commandments*. And *Ben-Hur*, too. Steve, that's Charlton Heston!"

"I don't believe it," Steve whispered. "Larry, we've got to get out of here!"

Just then a hotel attendant came along and asked, in that unmistakable tone of voice, whether there was anything he could help us with. Yes, he said, that was Mr. Charlton Heston playing tennis. No, it would not be possible to have a word with him. If we had no further business in the area, would we be so kind as to . . . . We took the not-so-subtle hint and turned to leave. As we started the car and pulled away from the curb, I got the distinct impression in my spirit that our divine appointment was not yet finished.

We pulled out of the sweeping driveway, past the shining Mercedes and Rolls-Royces, and turned down a side street lined with beautiful mansions. We rounded another corner and there, right ahead of us, was a familiar ten-foot wall of ivy. The tennis court again! Only now I could see that the barrier of ivy wasn't unbroken. At one point there was a small chain link gate that opened onto the court. And this time there was no hotel attendant around to shoo us away.

Steve saw the gleam in my eye. "Larry," he pleaded, "you can't be serious. Let's get out of here!"

I stopped the car, reached into the glove compartment for a small tract that explained how to become a Christian, and hopped out the door. "I've got to, Steve," I said. "I've just got a feeling . . . ."

As I stood peering through the chain link fence, I could once again see Mr. Heston. As I watched him play—he was quite good—I began to lift him up to the Lord.

No sooner had I begun to pray than a tennis ball careened off the side of his racket and sailed up toward a tall pine tree that grew alongside the court. It caromed from branch to branch—and then plopped right into my outstretched hands.

There was, of course, another player on the court, and two hotel attendants nearby. Probably one of them will jog over and retrieve the ball, I thought.

But no. As I stood there, mouth agape, feet frozen to the ground, tennis ball still clutched in outstretched hands, Heston trotted over to me.

My face probably matched his white tennis shirt and shorts as he peered at me through the fence. There I stood, eyeball to eyeball with the man who had split the Red Sea! I said the only thing that came to mind. "Ah, Mr. Heston, sir, well . . . could I have your autograph?"

He smiled as he scribbled his name on a scrap of paper.

"Oh, and this little leaflet is for you," I said, suddenly remembering the tract I had taken from the glove compartment a few moments before. I wedged it sideways through the fence. "When you take a break later, maybe you could check it out?"

"Sure." He stuffed the tract in his pocket. Then, after a brief pause, he looked at me with eyebrows raised and said, "Could I have the tennis ball, please?"

"Oh! Sure!" I said. I had forgotten all about it. I lobbed the ball up and over the fence, said goodbye, and headed back to the car. Steve was sitting inside, shaking his head in utter amazement.

I would love to be able to tell you that Charlton Heston called me the next day to tell me how my tract had revolutionized his life. But that didn't happen. To be quite honest, I don't know what effect our encounter may have had on him. But I *do* know that God had providentially arranged for our paths to cross and that my attentiveness to the prompting of the Spirit, plus the fact that I was prepared in advance for just such an eventuality, had enabled me to take advantage of the opportunity to witness to my faith.

Once we have had our own initial divine appointment with Jesus Christ, he works through us to reach people with the good news. When we become Christians we become part of a worldwide army of men and women being supernaturally guided by the Holy Spirit into contact with others. Sometimes we are able to bring another person to conversion. At other times, we are used to "plant a seed," or to be part of a series of contacts that may eventually lead to conversion. What makes evangelism exciting is knowing that we are not on our own but that we are continually carried along by God's Spirit into strategic encounters with unbelievers on a daily basis. This makes our mission an adventure, not a drudgery. These are the divine appointments that await us each day, if we are receptive to them.

The coast guard has a motto: *semper paratus.* That's Latin for "always prepared." It reflects the coast guard's commitment to be continuously on the alert and at the ready, prepared to go into action at a moment's notice.

We Christians are also supposed to be "always prepared." In his first letter, Peter urges his readers: "Always be prepared to give an answer to everyone who asks you to give the reason for the hope that you have" (1 Pt 3:15).

Peter is writing to Christians who are suffering great difficulty and persecution. He assumes that even in the midst of their troubles, their lives will be characterized by the hope, peace, and joy of the Holy Spirit, so much so that others will come to them and ask, "What's your secret?"

Christians today can be the same way. We who know the love of God and who are pursuing God's special calling on our lives can live such a vital, vibrant faith that friends, neighbors, co-workers—even complete strangers—come up to us and say, "There's something different about you. What is it?" There's something magnetic about a man or woman who is moving in God's plan and aggressively reaching out for his or her destiny.

But, of course, we are not to "just sit and wait" until someone asks us before we share about the Lord. Peter emphasizes the importance of being ready to witness to our faith at all times, to all people, under all circumstances. He understood that. That's because Peter knows that the Christian life is filled with divine appointments: opportunities to share the gospel with just the right person at just the right time. They may seem like random encounters, but in fact they have been carefully arranged and orchestrated by the Holy Spirit.

Many Christians don't have faith that God is sovereignly arranging divine appointments for them. Yet it is the will of God that we move in faith daily, realizing that God will use us and that he will regularly bring needy people our way.

What an exciting way to live! To think that the grand architect of the universe is strategically arranging our steps every day!

Recently I boarded a plane for Orlando, Florida, and discovered that Johnny Unitas, one of professional football's all-time greats, was also on board. He was in the first seat and as I waited for passengers to move forward, I recognized him.

"Excuse me," I said quietly. "Are you Johnny Unitas?"

"Yes, that's right."

We shook hands and I asked where he was headed.

I then reached into my sportcoat pocket and withdrew a colorful tract that contains my Christian testimony and a concise explanation of how one becomes a Christian by yielding his life to the Lordship of Jesus Christ. Handing it to him, I said, "It was good to meet you. Since this is a two hour flight, maybe you could check out this little leaflet. It tells the entire story of my life in about three minutes."

"Thanks," he nodded curiously.

Walking down the aisle I prayed, "Lord, if he doesn't know you personally, please open his heart to your good news of salvation."

Two hours later, upon landing in Florida I mentioned to the elderly gentleman seated next to me that Johnny Unitas was on the plane.

"Yes, I know," the man said. "He lives only a mile away from my house."

Out of all the passengers on a completely full flight I was seated next to someone who was able to share with me some insights into the person I had just evangelized. The whole experience impressed upon me that in the kingdom of God, there is no such thing as a chance encounter, only divine appointments.

Richard Parke, an evangelical minister who recently returned from missionary work in Greece, tells this story in a 1982 edition of *Christianity Today* magazine. In a letter to friends, he described events during a bus trip he took from California to Washington, D.C., in March 1981:

In Salt Lake City I transferred to an express bus that had arrived from Los Angeles. I picked out an empty seat next to a young man named John who became my seatmate for the next 1,000 miles of our journey.

Naturally we talked about many subjects as we rolled along mile after mile, but the Holy Spirit gave me the courage and the opportunity to talk to John specifically about eternal matters. He had attended church as a child but had drifted in recent years. He asked me what it meant to be "born again."

During the many hours together, I had opportunity to share my own story of coming to Jesus Christ almost eighteen years ago. I spoke with John about his own need for Christ and about God's love and forgiveness. And although there was little outward response on John's part, he listened to me.

Well, we got off the bus together in Washington, D.C., around noon on March 29, then claimed our baggage and said our goodbyes. And these were my parting words . . . 'John, I believe God had a reason for us to meet.'

Next day, I was shocked and saddened—as you were, too—to learn of the attempted assassination of President Reagan. Later that same afternoon, while looking at the TV screen, I noticed a still photograph of the alleged assassin. It was John W. Hinckley, Jr., my seatmate on the Greyhound bus!

Patrick Lowry is a friend of mine who makes his living painting and repairing houses. One day, as he was working on a house in the Beverly Hills area, he noticed a young woman who seemed to be having car trouble. She asked if he could help her, and Patrick climbed down from his ladder, raised the hood of her very flashy sports car, and tinkered with the battery until he was able to get the car to start.

The young woman, grateful for his assistance, asked if she could give him some money. Or perhaps she could thank him by taking him out for lunch?

Patrick, who knows a divine appointment when he sees one, chose the lunch.

As they drove off to the restaurant, Patrick turned to speak to the woman. She was wearing some rather plain clothes, but the numerous rings, bracelets, and necklaces she wore, not to mention the car she was driving, seemed to indicate someone of considerable wealth.

"My name's Patrick," he smiled. "Patrick Lowry. What's your name?"

The young lady glanced at him curiously. "Are you kidding me?" she asked.

"No, my name really *is* Patrick Lowry," he replied. "Who are you?"

"You mean you don't recognize me? You don't know who I am?"

Patrick was beginning to feel a little awkward. Should he recognize the young woman seated next to him? He searched his Hollywood memory banks. A movie star? Someone in a big television series? He just couldn't place her.

"No. I'm sorry. Who are you?"

"I'm Madonna!" she laughed.

"Oh," said Patrick. "Madonna who?"

Poor Patrick! He was too out of touch with the rock music scene to realize he was riding in a car with the biggest recording star of the year. Fortunately, he *was* enough in touch with the Holy Spirit to share his testimony and give her his personal life story, written up in a tract. She didn't seem too interested. But Patrick knew God had arranged some very unusual circumstances to enable him to plant a seed that could be watered at a later date.

I should point out that there is a difference between *evangelism* and *soul-winning*. Evangelism simply means sharing the gospel. Soul-winning refers to actually bringing a person to the point of conversion. Not all of our divine appointments lead to a conversion, but they all offer an opportunity to share about Jesus.

Dwight L. Moody, the famous evangelist, said, "I have never led a person to Jesus who had not been previously contacted with the gospel." In fact, someone has said that the average convert to Christianity has seven different exposures to the gospel before making a decision for Christ. When you are talking to someone about Jesus, you never know where they are at in the process. Your conversation might make it "one down, six to go." Then again, it just might be "six down ..." You have to be ready for anything.

I once heard a true story of a divine appointment that occurred precisely at the "six down, one to go" stage. A young Christian named Mark had made it a weekly practice to hand out gospel tracts door to door. One day he stopped at a house and rang the bell. No answer. Mark could hear muffled sounds coming from inside, indicating that someone was indeed home. So he kept ringing.

After several rings, a man finally threw open the door, took the tract Mark offered, and slammed the door before Mark even had a chance to wish him a nice day. Mark prayed God would open his heart to the gospel message and moved along to the next house.

A week later, Mark made a follow-up visit to the same neighborhood. He hesitated at the house where he had been so rudely received the week before but finally took a deep breath and rang the doorbell.

This time the man answered almost immediately and, to Mark's surprise, welcomed him enthusiastically. The man practically dragged Mark inside and up the steps to the attic. What Mark saw there took his breath away. There, dangling from an overhead rafter, was a length of stout rope with a noose tied at the end of it and a wooden box on the floor beneath it.

"Friend," the man said excitedly, "when you rang my doorbell last week, my head was in that noose. I was ready to kill myself. But you were so persistent ringing the bell that I decided to go downstairs and see who it was. I decided to read that little pamphlet you gave me because the title was so unusual. God used it to speak to me. Instead of jumping off that box, I knelt down beside it and gave my life to Jesus Christ. You saved my life."

Not all divine appointments are that dramatic. But whether dramatic or not, they happen all the time. Over the years, in addition to the hundreds of "ordinary" people to whom I have witnessed in this way, I have "bumped into" one former President of the United States, three pro football quarterbacks, the president of my alma mater (with whom I had shared my testimony fourteen years earlier!), two nationally known newscasters, several rock music stars, and, as I described earlier, one of Hollywood's most respected actors.

Why do these kinds of experiences come my way? First of all, because I expect them to! I know how heavily the preaching of the gospel weighs on God's heart. I know how insistent he is about seeing us fulfill the Great Commission. I know how eager he is to bring his servants into contact with those whose hearts he has prepared to hear the message of salvation. And so, as his obedient servant, I simply expect that he will be arranging divine appointments for me, maneuvering me into situations and circumstances in which I can share about him.

Whenever I am with another person for more than a few moments and in a situation where friendly conversation is possible, I try to ask myself, "Is this a divine appointment? Does God want me to share the good news in a relevant way with this person?" Most often, the answer is yes. Or if time doesn't permit, I simply give them my personal testimony tract (which I had printed years ago) and invite them to "check out my whole life's story in just three minutes." After over a decade of sharing my faith like this, I have only had about ten or twelve people turn me down. About ten thousand have either listened or taken home the intriguing little tract.

The second reason why I believe God leads me into so many such encounters is that he knows I'm ready. I'm always prepared to share the gospel with any one, any time, any place. And not just sports heroes and movie stars, by the way. The overwhelming majority of my evangelistic experiences have been with classmates, neighbors, family members, or "just plain folks" with whom God has brought me into contact.

What does it mean to be prepared to share? First of all, it means understanding the basic gospel message and being practiced at articulating it in a form that can be understood quickly and easily. There are many standard gospel presentations. Perhaps the best known is "The Four Spiritual Laws," developed by Campus Crusade for Christ or "The Two Question Test" from Frances Anfuso's Glad Tidings

School of Evangelism. Another is "The Bridge Diagram," popularized by the Navigators. I encourage you to learn one of these standard presentations or to develop one of your own. Practice with a friend until you can deliver it confidently, clearly, and quickly.

Second, learn how to share what the Lord has done in your own life. "The man with an experience," someone has said, "has it all over the man with an argument." Giving your personal testimony is often the easiest and most effective way to share about Christ. And it's easy to do. Take out a sheet of paper and divide it into three sections. In the top section, jot down some of the more noteworthy aspects of your life before you gave your life to the Lord. In the middle section, recall a few of the key thoughts and events that went into your decision to become a Christian. In the third section, list a few of the most significant things Jesus has done in your life since you became his disciple. There, in a nutshell, is your testimony.

Again, hone your presentation and practice with a friend until you can present it easily and naturally in about three minutes. Of course you *could* take hours telling your life story, but you will seldom have hours to talk to a new acquaintance about Christ. Three minutes is plenty for starters; if God grants the opportunity, you can always come back and fill in the details later.

Avoid Christian jargon that makes little sense to the unconverted. "Are you saved?" ("What's he talking about?"); "Been redeemed?" ("Does he mean green stamps?"); "Follow the Lamb" ("I like beef"); "You need to get committed" ("To a mental hospital?"). Sometimes, as in my encounter with Charlton Heston, you don't have even three minutes in which to share. For these occasions, it is very helpful to have your personal testimony in printed form. An individual may well be more attentive to your message if he or she can read it and reflect on it in private. Besides, you may find that handing someone a piece of paper is less frightening than starting a conversation with them, especially when you are just getting started.

I know what some of you are thinking. "Tracts! Give me a break! You mean those shabby-looking scraps of paper with unappealing messages like 'Are You Saved?' plastered across the front?" Well, no, not exactly. I mean attractive, colorful, relevant presentations of an individual's life story, with titles like, "I Was Fast Approaching My Goal of $144,000," "The Life of a P.O.W. (Prisoner of Want)," "Snatched from the Brink of Suicide," and "Is There Life after Rock'n'Roll?" These are titles of actual tracts, written by people I know who have accepted the challenge to be "always prepared" for evangelism and are seeing the results.

My wife's tract is headlined, "Is It Possible to Start Again?" On the front is a photo of Doris from before her conversion; she looks hard, her eyes seem empty. On the back is a more recent family portrait; the change in her appearance is unmistakable. Her story, which is reprinted in the appendix to this book, is inside. Feel free to use it as a model.

Over the years I have seen many people brought into relationship with Jesus because someone shared the good news with them in this simple but effective way.

Our Christian journey begins and continues with divine appointments. Are you alert to such encounters as you go about your daily routine? Are you prepared for them when they occur? Or does spiritual lockjaw suddenly develop, preventing you from capitalizing on God-arranged opportunities?

We need to be prepared for divine appointments. "Be wise in the way you act toward outsiders," Paul urges us. "Make the most of every opportunity" (Col 4:5). How about you? Are you prepared to make the most of the opportunities God brings to you?

The great escape artist, Houdini, understood the importance of preparation and timing. But on one occasion, he wasn't prepared. History records the tragic results.

Houdini was a remarkable artist who left the masses gasping at his performances. Once he escaped from a crate bound with chains at the bottom of New York Harbor. He burrowed his way out of graves and squirmed out of strait-jackets while hanging suspended in mid-air. He even freed himself from sturdy ropes that bound him to a stake while kerosene burned around him. His metal-like fingers and iron-nerved personality made him appear invulnerable.

One day, answering a dare, he allowed a boxer to hit him full force in the stomach. But his timing was a split second off and the boxer's fist slammed into him before he had prepared himself.

Houdini reeled but managed to regain his posture. "Not that way," he coughed, "I've got to get set. Now hit me."

The boxer hit again, smashing his fist against a seemingly granite abdomen.

Ten days later, the great Houdini died from the injury inflicted by the boxer's first blow. He had not been sufficiently prepared.

"Always be prepared to give an answer to everyone who asks you to give the reason for the hope that you have" (1 Pt 3:15).

Are you beginning to catch the spirit of one who lives life to the hilt by expecting divine appointments on a daily basis?

Or are you, perhaps, still one of those people who believes that evangelism is for others, but not for you? If so, read on. God has news for you!

FIVE

Evangelism Is for Everyone

HAS IT EVER HAPPENED TO YOU?

It's a weekday morning. You have just gotten the kids off to school and the breakfast dishes put away and the furniture pulled out from the wall so you can vacuum the carpet when there's a knock at the door. There on the front porch stand two clean-cut young men in dark suits and crisp white shirts. "Good morning," one of them smiles. "We're from the church of Jesus Christ of Latter-day Saints."

It's a Saturday afternoon. You have just finished hauling a load of neighborhood kids back from Little League practice. The hose is running and the bucket is filled with soapsuds and the car is in the driveway waiting to be washed when two middle-aged ladies stroll up the front walk. They ask you where you go to church and whether you'd be interested in talking about spiritual matters. You glance at the supply of magazines they have tucked under their arms: *The Watchtower*.

Once when I was speaking at a conference in England to about three thousand people, I asked how many in the audience had ever been proselytized by a Mormon or a Jehovah's Witness. Virtually everyone in the auditorium raised their hands. Then I asked how many had ever been personally contacted by a Christian who was not already an acquaintance.

About seventy people raised their hands.

Seventy out of three thousand! I would like to think that the group I was talking to was not typical of the general population. But I'm afraid it was. I have seen surveys showing that almost ninety percent of all church-going Christians have never led another person to Christ. If only ten percent of the church is evangelizing, no wonder so little evangelizing is getting done!

I am not saying we should copy the techniques of the Mormons or the Jehovah's Witnesses. But I *am* saying we all need to do our part, as "ambassadors for Christ," to obey the Great Commission (not the Great Suggestion) and evangelize the lost. We all need to be ready to share the good news in a natural and loving way as the Holy Spirit gives us opportunities. In addition, we need to support church-based ministries that spread the gospel, both overseas and here at home. We all need to become intercessors, to "pray the Lord of the harvest to send out laborers into his harvest," in order that "all may be saved and come to a knowledge of the truth." Whatever form it may take at any given time, the basic principle remains the same: evangelism is for everyone.

Today, as our Lord Jesus prepares us for a visitation of his Spirit and the ultimate restoration of his church, he is emphasizing more strongly than ever the primacy of evangelism. The same one who said, "Come unto me," also said, "Go into all the world." One of the reasons God redeems us is so that he can reach others through us. "I chose you," he tells us, "to go and bear fruit" (Jn 15:16). Notice how similar this is to God's very first command to the human race: "Be fruitful and increase in number" (Gn 1:28). His will for us hasn't changed.

All three synoptic gospels end on this insistent note of evangelism. "Go and make disciples of all nations" (Mt 28:19). "Go into all the world and preach the good news to all creation" (Mk 16:15). "Repentance and forgiveness of sins will be preached in his name to all nations" (Lk 24:47). The book of Acts takes up where the gospels leave off: "You will receive power when the Holy Spirit comes on you, and you will be my witnesses . . . to the ends of the earth" (Acts 1:8).

Why did Jesus come to earth in the first place? As he himself expressed it, "The Son of Man came to seek and to save what was lost" (Lk 19:10). "Here is a trustworthy saying that deserves full acceptance," Paul emphasizes. "Christ Jesus came into the world to save sinners" (1 Tm 1:15).

What did the first followers of Jesus do? They "went out and preached everywhere, and the Lord worked with them and confirmed his word by the signs that accompanied it" (Mk 16:20). They did their part, and the Lord did his. It still works that way today.

What then are you and I to do? We are to go into the *highways* (to those who are easy to reach) and the *hedges* (to those we must work to seek out) and "urge them to come in" (see Lk 14:23).

Seems pretty clear, doesn't it? Then why are so few of us doing it? What is it that holds us back from following the Lord's example, drawing on the power of his Spirit, and obeying his command? Why do so many of us have such a hang-up about evangelism? I can think of several common reasons:

Procrastination. Procrastination means putting off until tomorrow what we have already put off until today. Many of us know we are supposed to be evangelizing, but we "just haven't gotten around to it yet." The disciples seem to have had this same problem, and Jesus had sharp words for them: "Do you not say, 'Four months more and then the harvest'? I tell you, open your eyes and look at the fields! They are ripe for harvest" (Jn 4:35). Paul's words to the Corinthians can also be applied to us in this regard: "I tell you, *now* is the time of God's favor, *now* is the day of salvation" (2 Cor 6:2).

Discouragement. Some of us may be disheartened by the results of shallow evangelistic endeavors we have seen, or participated in, in the past. An emphasis on making decisions instead of making *disciples* amounts to preaching a watered-down gospel and does little to stir our faith and zeal for continued effort. Or we may have been turned off by gimmicks ("Bring-A-Bunch Night"), slick public relations campaigns, or mechanical formulas for evangelism that lack spiritual power.

Letting George Do It. Many Christians look upon evangelism as a specialized ministry reserved for those with a unique gift and calling. Some believers do have such a gift. But the fact remains that we are all called to be witnesses to the gospel. We may not have the *ministry gift* of evangelism (see Eph 4:11), but we are all called to "do the work of an evangelist" as the Spirit leads us (see 2 Tm 4:5). We are not supposed to be up in the stands watching but down on the field playing the game!

The "Silent Witness" Fallacy. Joe and Mike had worked together on the same job for years when Mike became a Christian. When he told Joe the good news, Joe replied, "I've been a believer for years. Didn't you know?" Mike answered, "You're the main reason I didn't become a Christian sooner! I thought, 'He's so good, why does a person need God?'" Obviously the way we live our lives is meant to witness to the grace and power of God. But demonstration without proclamation isn't enough.

Weariness. Many new Christians throw themselves into a frenzied evangelistic fervor, dropping "gospel bombs" and becoming "tract stars" for Jesus. When fatigue inevitably sets in, they slip into passivity. They not only need to recover their lost zeal, they also need help developing a Christian lifestyle that can sustain them in their service.

Sometimes this kind of weariness with evangelism comes from a different source. Some Christians come from backgrounds where there is great emphasis on preaching about evangelism but little emphasis on the pastor "equipping the saints for the work of ministry" (see Eph 4:12). As a result, they become "dull of hearing" and never get up out of the pew and into action.

Imbalance. One extremely common trap is to become imbalanced in emphasizing "building up the church" to the neglect of reaching the lost. We comfort ourselves with the rationalization that we can't evangelize until we are "mature enough." Our desire not to upset the apple cart ("But we just got our home groups in order!") becomes an excuse for not fulfilling our responsibility to lost humanity. Spirit-led planning, discipling, and leadership development are important. But we must not pursue them to the exclusion of evangelism.

Pride. Some of us smugly view evangelism as "elementary"—good for fired-up new believers but beneath us now that we are mature. Our quest for "the deep things of God" becomes a rationalization for disobedience to the Great Commission. Or perhaps we tell ourselves that our call is to be "prophetic" more than "evangelistic." That may be true to some extent. But what does it mean to be prophetic, after all? It means being tuned in to what God is feeling, thinking, and saying. And the redemption of lost humanity is *always* on God's heart, especially in the critical hour in which we live.

Koinonitis. The Greek word for "fellowship" is *koinonia*. Sometimes churches and individuals so desire to preserve accustomed patterns of Christian fellowship and so enjoy each other's company that they slowly lose the vision for reaching the lost. It can happen to anybody. Dr. C. Peter Wagner, professor at Fuller Theological Seminary, the church growth expert, calls this condition "koinonitis." Where it strikes, people often develop a theology to justify abandoning outreach: "Small is beautiful." "We're after quality, not quantity" (actually, according to Scripture we're supposed to be after both). "Jesus said, 'Where two or three are gathered . . . .'" They feel threatened by anything that might break up their "holy huddle." This infection is subtle and can become terminal. It must be recognized and resisted like the plague.

"The Flesh Is Weak." God doesn't intend for us to evangelize in our own strength. Scripture makes clear that the Holy Spirit is given to us precisely to empower and embolden us. Some of us may need to learn how to rely more on the Spirit within us and less upon our own resources; others may not yet have truly experienced being baptized in the Spirit.

Lack of Instruction. I continually run into Christians who know they should be involved in evangelism and who even feel vaguely guilty because they are not. Their problem? They have never been taught *how* to go about it. Evangelism is not *mainly* a matter of technique, but some basic knowledge and training is indispensable.

It is particularly helpful to know how to respond to some of the objections people commonly raise when confronted with the gospel. It helps us: being equipped with clear answers to legitimate questions and objections helps us overcome the fear of being "stumped," a fear that is a powerful deterrent to witnessing. And, of course, it helps the people with whom we share: Spirit-led answers, based on the truth of God's word, give the Holy Spirit an opportunity to enlighten minds that are "blinded by the god of this age" (see 2 Cor 4:2-4). Here are a few of the more familiar objections, with suggestions on how to respond to them drawn from my experience and that of many of the leaders with whom I serve.

"What about the people who've never heard about Jesus Christ?" First, we must point out that God is just. Romans 2:14-15 clearly indicates that every person has a conscience and has been granted some measure of revelation regarding what is right and what is wrong. If a person has never received the full revelation or even heard of our Lord Jesus Christ, I believe with Dr. Billy Graham that they will be judged according to the light they do have.

We should note that God promises to reward all those who "diligently seek him" (Heb 11:6) and that he can supply his grace to any earnest seeker, anywhere, at any time, even on the remotest island or the most obscure regions of Mongolia.

But we must also bring the focus of attention back from those who have never heard the gospel to the person with whom we are talking. The issue for him is not what will happen to those who have not heard, but what he will do with what he *has* heard.

"How do you know God exists?" Who has ever heard of an invention that has no inventor? Common sense tells us the neatly ordered rows of corn in a roadside field didn't arrange themselves; the same logic applies when we observe the planets ordered in their orbits around the sun. The psalmist declares, "The heavens are telling the glory of God" (Ps 19:1). The very design of the universe around us points to the existence of a Designer.

For a person who finds this line of thinking unpersuasive, share the "circle of knowledge" illustration. Draw a large circle to represent all the knowledge in the universe. Have him draw another circle inside it, representing the amount of this total knowledge he personally holds. Then ask, "Is it possible that God does indeed exist but that his existence is unknown to you—that it falls outside your personal circle of knowledge?" If he will admit this possibility, he has changed from an atheist to an agnostic, and he may now be in a better position to hear the remainder of your presentation.

"Is Jesus the only way to God?" Sometimes people argue that sincerity is what matters most, regardless of whether one is a Hindu, a Moslem, or a Christian. Point out that one can be utterly sincere but still be desperately wrong. A person might believe quite sincerely that he could live forever without ever eating or drinking again. But if he sincerely pursues this conviction, he will be pushing up daisies before too long!

Also, defuse the underlying accusation that Christians are bigoted for believing that Jesus is the only way. We are not bigoted, we are faithful. It was Jesus who said, "I am *the* Way"; as honest Christians, how can we do anything but repeat his claim?

"The Bible is full of contradictions and hard to under-stand." First, in a gentle spirit, ask them to point out some contradictions. They will probably not be able to do so. Most people who raise this objection have never read the Bible for themselves; they are simply parroting a common misconception.

If they do bring up something that appears contradictory, don't evade their question. Answer as honestly and thoroughly as you can. If you are unable to respond adequately at the moment, offer to do some study and get back to them later.

As to the Bible being "too hard to understand," consider the following: If a person is referring to the book of Revelation, with its imagery and prophetic pictures, he has a point. But how hard is it to understand the simple gospel message as presented in John 3:16?

"If God is good and all-powerful, why is there evil and suffering?" This question presupposes that all the evil and suffering in the world (war, poverty, sickness) is God's fault: either God is not all-good because he allows evil to continue, or he is not all-powerful because he is unable to prevent it from happening. We must point out that evil exists and persists because human beings have rebelled against God and have chosen to go their own way. Man's selfishness, greed, and pride have caused the world's woes. God could, of course, have made us in such a way that we could not help but obey him and do good. But then we would be robots, not truly human; God's desire is not for robots but for beings who can love him by free choice.

"Do you really believe in a literal hell?" Yes. Jesus spoke of hell more frequently than he did of heaven. Hell is a real place and a place of real torment (see Lk 16:19-31). But it is important to make clear that God did not originally intend for human beings to go to hell. Hell was created for the devil and his angels (Mt 25:41). Men and women go to hell only when they refuse to accept God's free gift of eternal life and, in effect, cast their lot with the devil.

"How do you know Jesus rose from the dead?" There have been many arguments trying to deny the bodily resurrection of Jesus. From the very beginning, the lie was spread that the disciples stole Jesus' body (Mt 28:11-15). Today, many people believe the early Christians made up the whole story. There are two strong pieces of evidence against this contention. First, why would men die—ten of the original twelve disciples were martyred—bearing witness to a story they knew to be false? Second, you, like countless thousands of others, have had your life transformed, not by some theory or philosophy but by the power of the risen Christ. Your personal testimony is irrefutable.

"Is Jesus God?" The Scriptures clearly present Jesus as God the Son (Heb 1:1-3, 8), as God eternal (Jn 1:1), as great God and Savior (Ti 2:13), and as God worthy of worship (Jn 20:28). As C.S. Lewis has observed, Jesus was either a liar, a lunatic, or the Lord of all. As we consider his sinless life, his matchless miracles, and his unequalled wisdom, it is beyond doubt that Jesus substantiated his claim to be the great "I Am" (John 8:58; see also Ex 3:14).

"The church is full of hypocrites!" Unfortunately, this may be all too true. But this fact does not invalidate the reality of Jesus Christ. Note that Jesus' strongest denunciations were directed at the religious hypocrites of his own day. What is important is to focus on the person of Christ, not on those who follow him imperfectly.

"Won't being a good person get me to heaven?" God doesn't grade on the curve. His standard is not relative; his standard is absolute perfection. Certainly some of us are "better people" than others (any of us would win a "good person contest" if our competition were Adolf Hitler or Charles Manson). But none of us is perfect, and thus none of us qualifies on his own merits. We can't save ourselves. We need outside help. That's why God sent Jesus.

"There are no absolutes!" A simple question in reply

should suffice: "Are you *absolutely* sure?"

Remember the following points as you engage in discussion over these and other topics:

—Avoid arguments and foolish questions (2 Tm 2:24).

—You are not "The Answer Man." If you don't know the answer to a question, admit it and offer to find out the answer. Your honesty will accomplish more than a razzle-dazzle response.

—Treat your inquirer and his questions with respect and genuine interest.

—Walk in the Spirit. Our battle is not merely intellectual, it is spiritual. Only the Holy Spirit is able to convict and convert the minds and hearts of men.

As we consider the various reasons why so many Christians fail to evangelize, let's be honest with ourselves before God. We should take inventory of our attitudes and repent for any ways in which we have rationalized or excused ourselves from our biblical responsibility. As Christian leader Stephen Olford has said, "It is characteristic of our natural sluggishness and laziness to put off the work of evangelism. By cunning calculations and clever rationalizations, we talk ourselves out of the urgency of the task and the demand upon our time, talents, and treasures. How we need to ask the Holy Spirit to rid us of all unbelief, indifference, prejudice, and hard-heartedness."

As we prepare to launch out in evangelism, we should ask the Lord to purify our motives. Paul said, "We are not trying to please men but God, who tests our hearts" (1 Thes 2:4). Our motive must be to please God and bring delight to his heart (see Lk 15:7), not just to salve our guilt, impress our leaders, or bring recognition to ourselves.

Let's ask the Lord to sensitize us to the divine appointments sovereignly arranged for us each day. Let's also ask him to impart his compassion to us that we may feel in our hearts the hurt and pain he experiences over the fallen state of the human race he created. Jesus wept over Jerusalem and grieved at the spiritual sickness of his people. Paul was willing to exchange his own salvation if by doing so his kinsmen could be saved. Moses pleaded that his own name be blotted out for the sake of God's mercy on his people. Not driven by guilt but inspired by love, let's move forward to make every day a masterpiece for God. Watch how he will honor obedience with thrilling testimonies of appointments having been fulfilled.

SIX

It'll Work for You, Too!

H IGH SCHOOL GRADUATION. I could still remember it as if it were yesterday: standing on stage, wearing a gown that felt too long and a cap that felt too small, doing my best to stay awake through the commencement address. Four hundred of us in all, shaking hands with the principal while receiving the long-awaited diploma. Singing "The Impossible Dream" as the ceremony came to an end. . . .

Had it really been fourteen years?

I was back in Cleveland, visiting my old stomping grounds. You probably know the feeling: you're surprised that everything looks the same after so many years, and yet . . . you can't put your finger on it, but somehow everything seems different. Changed. Older. Or is it *you* that has changed?

"There's 'Bob's,'" I thought to myself as I drove past the familiar burger-and-fries restaurant down the street from my old high school. "We used to hang out there all the time . . . after baseball practice, after all the dances . . . . Maybe I'll go in and get a Coke, just for old times' sake."

The years had taken their toll on Bob's. The plastic seat covers, once bright and colorful, were now faded and cracked with age. The flooring had been replaced, and the new stuff didn't quite go with the color of the drapes. Even "Bob" himself—a statue out in front of the restaurant—needed a fresh coat of paint.

"Where is everybody?" I thought, as memories of bygone gatherings and faces flashed back in my mind. I used to be able to walk in and recognize half the faces in the restaurant. Now, there was nobody I knew in the place. Except . . .

"Hey! Larry! Larry Tomczak! Is that you?"

The voice came from a young man seated alone in a corner booth. Underneath the beard and the long hair I recognized a fellow from my graduating class.

"John! It's been a long time. How've you been?"

"Not bad, Larry, not bad at all. Man, it's been years! Here, have a seat."

I slid into the booth, across from my old classmate. I hadn't known him very well, and aside from exchanging the usual pleasantries there didn't seem to be much for us to talk about.

"Say, John, do you see many of the guys from our class any more?"

"Oh, sometimes. A few of them are still around. You know," he smirked, "it seems like most of the guys from our class wound up in one of four places."

Taking a sip of my Coke, I glanced up at him, curious about what he would say.

"I may be off," he began, "but it seems to me everybody's either on drugs and divorced, in jail, already dead, or . . ." his voice trailed off.

"Or what?" So far, John's assessment seemed obviously exaggerated and more than a little sarcastic.

"Well, a bunch of them have become these 'born-again' religious types."

That certainly caught my attention. If this wasn't a "divine appointment," I didn't know what was. But I wasn't quite sure what to say next. So I did the only thing that seemed logical under the circumstances: I leaned back in the booth, drew a deep breath, and took another bite out of my onion ring.

"So, John," I finally said. "Tell me what's been going on with *you*."

John's mood changed almost instantly. He was pretty

cheerful as long as we were reminiscing about the good old days; he didn't seem so thrilled about discussing his own present situation. As he began talking, I could understand why. John had led a fairly dismal life since high school. He got heavily involved in drugs and had been arrested for possession. Now he was trying to improve his life and was coaching elementary school athletics. He warned his students "to avoid drugs like the plague," he said, even though he himself was still using them.

"Don't you ever feel a little hypocritical, saying one thing and living another?" I asked him.

For several moments he gazed out the plate-glass front window of the restaurant at the passing traffic, then shrugged his shoulders and mumbled something about being "kind of stuck in a trap."

I asked him some more questions. What about God? We had gone to a parochial school together, and he was coaching at one now. Did he believe in God? Had he ever asked God to help him? His response was discouraged and discouraging: "I don't know. I'm not sure God really exists."

"You know, John," I began slowly, "this may come as something of a surprise, but remember what you said earlier? About how some of the guys had become born-again Christians?"

"Yeah."

"Well, I'm one of them."

He glanced at me quickly, then turned his gaze away again.

"John, have you ever really thought about what Jesus could do for you if you gave him the chance?"

He didn't answer. After a few moments of awkward silence, he changed the subject. It was clear he didn't want to talk any more. But at least we had made a beginning. I left a copy of my personal testimony with him, and he promised that he would "take a look at it sometime."

I walked slowly back to my car, already praying that the Holy Spirit would move in John's heart, that what we had talked about and what he would read in the tract would help move him closer to the liberating power of Jesus Christ. As I backed out of my parking space, I could see him still sitting there by the window, slumped back in the drab restaurant booth, smoking a cigarette.

The whole encounter started me thinking. What about all the other guys in our class? Where were they at, spiritually speaking? I knew that some of them really were in bad shape, just as John had indicated. What about the others? I had to fight to hold back the tears. These were friends of mine! How would they all be reached with the gospel?

In the last chapter, I spoke primarily of the need so many believers have to take seriously their divine appointment to the office of ambassador for Christ. But there is another need that many of us have: the need for encouragement as we go about the task of spreading the gospel, especially with those closest to us. Many of us experience keenly the desire to see our family and friends come to know Jesus. We want to share the gospel with them, but we don't know where to begin, or we are afraid "it'll never work" for us. Wherever I travel, I hear statements like these from Christians who are concerned about someone close to them:

"Larry, my son has rejected his religious upbringing just like you did, and now he doesn't want to hear when I try to tell him about Jesus."

"My best friend is living with a man. She even had an abortion. What do I say to her?"

"My parents go to church, but they really don't seem to know Jesus in a personal way. How can I reach out to them?"

"My friends don't understand what's happened to me. How can I get through to them?"

Sometimes our God-given burden for those we love can bring us to a point of gnawing anxiety, even guilt. While God certainly wants us to be concerned for the spiritual well-being of our loved ones, he doesn't want us to be weighed down with worry. Rather, he wants us to approach this area with trust in him, knowing that he desires their salvation even more than we do and confident that he is at work in their lives.

My wife and I have seen this truth borne out in our own experience. Between us, we have seen eleven immediate family members come to know Jesus Christ personally in the last ten years. In addition, we have seen many of our friends—including, I should add, a number of old high school classmates—turn their lives over to Christ.

God can work in the lives of your loved ones, too. Here are some principles I have learned that will help you cooperate with the work of his Spirit:

Believe God's Word. We need to be absolutely convinced that God's word is true when it tells us that he "desires all men to be saved and to come to a knowledge of the truth" (1 Tm 2:4). Underline the *all*. There is no one whom God does not want to see brought to himself! That includes parents, children, old school friends, *everyone*.

"But Larry, you don't know my dad. He just walks away when I try to tell him about the Lord."

"But Larry, you don't know my roommate. He never wants to do anything but smoke pot and stay out all night. He just laughs at me and calls me a 'Jesus Freak.'"

You're right: I *don't* know all the particular "tough cases" in your life. But I *do* know that Jesus knows them, and loves them, and wants to bring them to himself. Jesus died for all, even for the most callous sinner, the one who seems hardest to reach.

Pray and Fast. The great Christian author J. Oswald Sanders has said, "It is doubtful that any person is saved apart from the believing prayers of some saint." It is vitally important that we "stand in the gap," praying for the salvation of our loved ones. Write their names down and lift them up to the Lord every day. See yourself as a spiritual warrior, calling down the powers of heaven against the blindness, the deception, the hardness of heart that surrounds them. As you do so, be alert to the possible influence of evil spirits—rebellion, deception, pride, intellectualism—and bind their work as Jesus commissioned us (see Mt 18:18-19).

Don't Forget God's Other Workers. Don't fall into the

trap of thinking you are the only one who can reach your friends and loved ones. Remember what Jesus said: "Ask the Lord of the harvest to send out workers into his harvest field" (Mt 9:38). As we pray for specific individuals, we can trust God to engineer situations in which his "field representatives" can come into contact with them. It's amazing how often God will use a work associate, a classmate, someone writing in a newspaper or magazine, a television personality, a radio evangelist, even a good samaritan who picks them up when their car breaks down (that's what happened to me!), to get through to them when you have been unable to do so.

Tangibly Express Your Love. This is one of the most important ways we witness to the transforming power of God in our lives. Talk is cheap. If we don't live it, we shouldn't lip it! We can most effectively earn the right to be heard by demonstrating a changed life. Look for ways to serve those you desire to reach.

When I first became a Christian, I very much wanted to share the gospel with my sister. She was skeptical about my having "gotten religious" and wary of discussing it with me. Small wonder! She had known me all my life, and most of the time I didn't exactly set a sterling example of unselfish love and sacrificial service. But when I invited her to join me for a vacation in Atlantic City, with me picking up the tab, she knew something had really changed! That opened the door. I was soon able to share with her and help her come to know Jesus.

Initiate Reconciliation. One of the problems in witnessing to those who have known us for a long time is that usually we've had our share of misunderstandings, negative speech, and hurtful behavior.

Reconciliation is a directive, not an elective; an action, not an emotion. Are there any unresolved offenses between you and any friends or family members? Get them straightened out. Take the initiative yourself, and focus on the part *you* have played in the situation. When my sister and I asked our parents to forgive us for being selfish, disrespectful, and rebellious, many barriers crumbled, clearing the way to their eventual conversion experience.

Hang In There. Perseverance is crucial in evangelism. Sometimes a person's receptivity enables God's work to move along rapidly, but often we will find ourselves engaged in a process that may extend over months or even years. The important thing is to "keep on keepin' on." Continue to do the things you know are right to do, and focus your attention on God's faithfulness rather than on the apparent lack of results in the present.

God wants the apostle Paul's magnificent obsession with evangelism to become ours as well. In Romans 1:14-16, he cites three "I am's" that relate to this point:

I am under obligation. In other words, evangelism is not just for volunteers. All of us are commissioned as "ambassadors for Christ." "Woe to me," Paul tells the Corinthians, "if I do not preach the gospel" (1 Cor 9:16).

I am eager to preach the gospel. This should be our attitude as well. Evangelism is an adventure, not a chore!

I am not ashamed of the gospel. We need never be intimidated at the prospect of sharing about Jesus or apologetic about our love for him. "He who is in you is greater than he who is in the world" (1 Jn 4:4).

I believe that the Lord Jesus is preparing us for a remarkable visitation of the Spirit in our day, to see his church restored and the world impacted by the gospel. As part of this, I believe he wants to re-emphasize the importance of Spirit-led evangelism. Here is how a group of Christian leaders from around the world expressed it in a solemn agreement called the Lausanne Covenant:

> We need to acknowledge that of all the tragic needs of human beings, none is greater than their alienation from their Creator and the terrible reality of eternal death for those who refuse to repent and believe. Rather than be guilty of an inexcusable lack of human compassion, we are privileged to commit ourselves with urgency to this task of evangelism.

In this critical hour of history, we must embrace our mandate and reject Satan's lie that people are not interested in what we have to offer. As conditions in society deteriorate, more and more people are becoming receptive to the message we declare and demonstrate. They don't want mere religion, they want reality: the kind of ultimate reality found only in Jesus Christ.

In this exciting time, when the Holy Spirit is beginning to be poured out, I believe we are seeing, and will continue to see, a new atmosphere of openness to the gospel. So don't let fear slow you down, and don't let temporary setbacks stop you in your tracks. You are part of an end-time army God is preparing, one that believes God is actively at work in their lives to reach the world. Spreading the gospel works—even for you!

Part III

Divine Appointment *from* God: Moving in the Miraculous

The Lord appointed seventy-two others and sent them two by two ahead of him. He told them, "Heal the sick and tell them, 'The kingdom of God is near to you.'" (Lk 10:1, 2, 9)

SEVEN

With Signs Following

I T WAS A SUNDAY MORNING like any other. Doris and I had loaded our four little ones in the car and rambled off to church. We arrived a bit early so the children could get settled and I could take care of a few last minute details before the service began.

Suddenly I heard a commotion in the meeting room, then footsteps pounding down the hall toward my office.

"Larry, come quickly!" The young man who stood in my doorway was out of breath and looked pale and frightened. "It's Doris's Dad. He's . . ."

I didn't wait to hear the rest. I raced back to the meeting room, where a small knot of people were huddled around the prostrate form of my father-in-law, who lay unconscious on the floor.

"He just collapsed, Larry. We can't rouse him," someone said. Doris and her mother were at Dad's side, praying over him.

As we waited for the ambulance to arrive, we laid hands on Dad, praying the "prayer of faith" (see Jas 5:15) and believing God for his complete healing.

Events raced ahead with the speed of a videotape player stuck in fast forward. The paramedics arrived and swiftly went into action. A nurse who attended our church clutched my arm, her face ashen. "I can't find a pulse, Larry," she whispered. As the paramedics began moving Dad's stretcher toward the door, Doris asked them, "Will my father make it?"

"It doesn't look good," one of them replied. "I'm sorry. It doesn't look good."

Doris accompanied her mother on the ambulance ride to the hospital, while I stayed to lead the church in prayer. We joined in declaring the promises of God concerning the healing of the sick. We prayed, asking God to fulfill these promises in Doris's father. Finally, focusing on God's faithfulness rather than on the unsettling natural circumstances, we lifted our voices in an anthem of thanksgiving and praise.

To this day we are not sure, medically speaking, what happened to Dad that Sunday morning. The paramedics assumed something serious had gone wrong with his heart. But the medical tests later showed nothing, and on the following Tuesday he was released from the hospital. On Saturday, less than a week after his frightening collapse, he went out and played his regular weekly round of golf.

As I said, we are still not really sure what happened medically. But we have no doubt what happened spiritually. *God healed him.* Doris and her parents and I and the whole church rejoiced at having been eyewitnesses to, even participants in, a miracle.

In these climactic hours in which God is restoring his church, he wants to show the world that he is truly alive, that he cares for people both spiritually and physically, and that he is able to do today what he did through his early church. He wants to demonstrate a gospel of power accompanied by signs and wonders. He is looking for a people who will fulfill this divine appointment to move in the miraculous just as his first disciples did.

The healing of my father-in-law is just one instance of something I have increasingly grown to expect over the years: the supernatural intervention of God. I have been privileged to witness and, on several occasions, to be God's instrument in numerous works of power: signs, wonders, healings, miracles.

I now look upon them as a normal part of the Christian life.

But it wasn't always that way. In fact, my first taste of the miraculous caught me unprepared.

It was 1974. I was one of the speakers at an event called "Jesus '74," an open-air festival near the rural town of Mercer, Pennsylvania. There were almost twenty thousand young people at the festival, spilling out the sides of the huge canvas tent and onto the surrounding hillside.

With that large a crowd of fired-up folks, I expected a high enthusiasm level. But as I began to speak I felt an electricity in the air that couldn't be accounted for merely by my preaching or by the youthful energy of the audience. The atmosphere in that tent couldn't have been more highly charged if it had been plugged into the main generator of a nuclear power plant.

The presence of the power of God could scarcely have been more pronounced. In the days and weeks that followed, the testimonies came in about what had happened that day. Deafness was healed. Crutches were discarded. A blind eye was restored. Longstanding ailments dissolved like snow in the August sun.

My response? I was completely overwhelmed. When the session ended I fought my way through the crowd and hurried back to my hotel room. Trembling, I dropped to my knees and poured out my heart to God. "Lord, I don't know if I'm equipped to handle this kind of thing," I said. "I mean, I want everything you have for me, and I give you all the glory for what you are doing, but I have to tell you honestly, I'm not sure I'm ready for this."

That may not have been the boldest prayer God ever heard, but it did mark the beginning of a more consistent experience of the intervention of God's power in my life and through my ministry. I have numerous letters in my files documenting healings that have taken place in response to prayer. In one corner of my office, I even have a small collection of canes cast aside by men and women who once were lame or crippled but now are thoroughly restored. And I have vivid memories of many individuals' divine appointments with God's sovereign power.

One of those memories concerns a man named Wesley. It happened several years ago in Tulsa. Wesley was an elderly man, a bit out of place in an auditorium filled with some 2,300 young people. He had suffered four major heart attacks and eight lesser ones and was taking massive doses of medication; in fact, his cardiologist had told Wesley he knew of only one recorded instance of a patient taking a higher dosage.

As the meeting progressed, I sensed the Holy Spirit speaking to me. "Larry, I want to miraculously heal Wesley tonight. Submit it to the leader of the meeting and have the people pray."

Inwardly I felt my heart sink. Frankly, there is still a part of me that shudders when God does things like that. That part of me immediately began reasoning with God: "But Wesley is so old. And he's been so sick for so long. Even now, he's visibly 'under the influence' of his medication. Besides [here came the real concern] there's a couple thousand people here. What if it doesn't work? My reputation is on the line!"

The inner impression intensified. I sensed this word in my spirit: "I want to miraculously heal Wesley tonight. Are you going to do what I asked you?"

Gulp.

I told the leader of the meeting what I had in mind. He explained it to the crowd and we began to pray. What happened next is best described by Wesley himself.

"When everyone agreed in prayer," he later recounted, "the Spirit of the Lord came upon me. It felt like getting struck by a bolt of lightning. I felt heat in my chest. Then I began rejoicing."

And well he might have rejoiced! Wesley experienced a miracle that night. Today, to the bafflement of his cardiologists, he rides a bike seven miles a day. He has testified to his healing in churches and on Christian radio and television programs nationwide.

That experience taught me a lesson I have tried never to forget: when God calls us into action in the supernatural, our response must simply be obedience, even when it isn't easy.

And often it *isn't* easy.

A couple years ago I was addressing a group of young people when I heard that familiar voice speaking to my spirit. The Holy Spirit was telling me there was a young girl in the audience who was pregnant and scheduled to have an abortion within the next week. I was to invite her to come forward, turn away from her decision to have an abortion, and ask for God's help in completing her pregnancy.

I paused in my presentation and shared the sense the Lord had given me: "There's a young lady here tonight—I'm not sure of your age—but you're pregnant and you're planning to get an abortion this week. God wants you to know that he loves you and he loves your baby and he wants to help you. He wants you to do a very brave thing. He wants you to come forward and accept his love and forgiveness and help." I waited a few moments. No response. (Devil: "You blew it, you idiot.")

I tried again.

Still no response. (Devil: "These people think you're crazy, you know.")

I took a deep breath and repeated the words a third time.

At last a young girl stood up and slowly made her way to the stage. That marked the beginning of a long and sometimes difficult process of counseling and pastoral support. But God was faithful. Today, a photo of a two-year-old boy rests in my desk drawer. I was privileged to assist in the adoption of this precious child, whose life was saved because of a divine appointment with God's love.

There have been many other times when I have responded to such a "word of knowledge" (see 1 Cor 12:8) and have seen great things happen. But I don't want to mislead you. It doesn't happen that way every time. On a few occasions I have stepped out in faith in just the same manner and seemed to miss the mark.

Of course, there is the possibility that the word of knowledge *was* accurate but that someone was just afraid to respond at the time. I have frequently had someone approach me after a session, in private, and say, "That word was for me." But sometimes I just plain miss it. When that happens, I try to remember Paul's words, "For we know in part and we prophesy in part" (1 Cor 13:9). I have simply decided to accept the fact that I will make mistakes but that I should obey and trust God for the outcome. I believe God is more pleased with us when we step out in faith and fail than when we sit back and do nothing for fear of failure. God can redeem our mistakes!

If we're going to keep the divine appointments God arranges for us, we are going to have to learn to move in the supernatural.

Jesus' life and ministry was filled with the miraculous, from his virgin birth through his resurrection and ascension.

The disciples' ministry was filled with the miraculous as Jesus "gave them power and authority to drive out all demons and to cure diseases, and he sent them out to preach the kingdom of God and to heal the sick" (Lk 9:1-2).

The life of the early church was characterized by miracles that upset religious systems and shook the Roman government to its foundations.

Paul testified to what he had "said and done—by the power of signs and miracles, through the power of the Spirit" (Rom 15:18-19).

Of Philip it is recorded, "When the crowds heard [him] and saw the miraculous signs he did, they all paid close attention to what he said. With shrieks, evil spirits came out of many, and many paralytics and cripples were healed" (Acts 8:6-7).

Stephen is called "a man full of God's grace and power

[who] did great wonders and miraculous signs among the people" (Acts 6:8).

The church of Jesus Christ was never intended to function purely on an earthly, natural plane. It is a supernatural organism, not just a natural organization. Remove the pages from the New Testament where miraculous activity is recorded or referred to, and there is almost nothing left. Remove the supernatural and Christianity loses its virility, its fascination. There is nothing left but empty religious forms and lifeless formality.

In Scripture, healings and miracles serve as *signs*: demonstrations of the reality and love and power of God, proofs to an unbelieving world that the message of the gospel is true.

They serve the same purpose in our time. The men and women of our generation are looking for reality. They want to see God in action. It's when they do not see the supernatural properly manifested in Christianity that they turn to Satan's counterfeits: spiritism, astrology, the occult, drug-induced experiences. All these cravings are perversions of an entirely appropriate human desire: the desire to experience the power of the living God.

World population is growing, some say, by 140,000 people a day. That's fifty million a year! The church's worldwide evangelistic task is enormous. And it will not be accomplished without the miraculous. Throughout Christian history, the most effective form of mass evangelism has always been signs and wonders. A single miracle is more valuable than a million dollars worth of advertising. It can disarm more skeptics than a library full of apologetics books.

In my files is a newspaper account of a miracle service in England in which I was privileged to be involved:

> The people stood and were applauding and thanking God. They had been cured of respiratory problems, headaches, migraines, problems with limbs and arthritis. A

number were running up and down the platform. They had had stiff legs for years and they now could bend them easily.

A photograph of the event appeared above the caption, "Cancer Cure," in dark, bold letters. I can't help but think that a few reserved, proper Englishmen juggled their teacups when they saw that!

Let's not settle for anything less than authentic New Testament Christianity, validated by the miracle-working power of the living God. Rather than relying solely on intellectual ability, let's follow the example of Paul, who reminded the Corinthians, "My message and my preaching were not with wise and persuasive words, but with a demonstration of the Spirit's power, so that your faith might not rest on men's wisdom, but on God's power" (1 Cor 2:4-5).

But isn't it selfish, or sensationalistic, to desire miracles and works of power? Absolutely not!

When Peter saw Jesus walking on the water, he wanted to do it, too! He wanted to experience the miraculous. Jesus didn't rebuke him, he encouraged him! It was only when Peter's faith later wavered that Jesus rebuked him.

Jesus said, "These signs will accompany *those who believe*: In my name they will drive out demons; they will speak in new tongues . . . they will place their hands on sick people, and they will get well" (Mk 16:17-18).

Are you a believer? Then God says it is his will that you be a conductor of his miraculous power.

In 1945, T.L. Osborne and his wife went to India as missionaries. His intention: to preach the gospel "with signs following." Traditional missionaries ridiculed his plan. They advised him to learn the language, be friendly, and expect no results for three years. He tried to apply their counsel, yet in time returned home a disillusioned young man. In his desperation he cried out to the Lord, who appeared to him and charged him, "Dare to act upon my word!" Osborne obeyed. For more than thirty years, in some seventy different countries, he has since seen God perform thousands of miracles to confirm the proclamation of the gospel.

"The love of the miraculous is not a mark of ignorance," Osborne insists. "Rather, it reveals man's intense desire to reach the unseen God."

Osborne's observations about much of modern-day Christianity are convicting:

- —The availability of the miraculous power of God and the gifts of the Holy Spirit are clearly taught in Scripture;
- —Because leaders don't know, don't believe, or don't preach these teachings, God's people are unaware of them;
- —If people don't know about these truths, they can scarcely have faith for them;
- —Where there is a climate of little or no faith, few miracles occur (see Mk 6:5-6);
- —When few or no miracles occur, there is little to draw unbelievers to God.

The results: God is robbed of his glory. Anointed preachers are robbed of powerful confirmation of their message. God's people are robbed of the full deliverance obtained on Calvary.

There is not a word in Scripture that says that miracles were used to help begin the church but are no longer available. The power of God is just as available as it ever was. The reason we experience so little of it is that the church, in many quarters, has grown lukewarm and content without it. Much of the church is like the pitiful town that Jesus visited: "He could not do any miracles there, except lay his hands on a few sick people and heal them. And he was amazed at their lack of faith" (Mk 6:5-6).

Today, as the Holy Spirit is raising the level of expectation for the miraculous, let's decide to stop offering the world a thimblefull of God's saving power. Let's cultivate the conviction, based on God's word, that moving in the miraculous can and should be a normal part of Christian life. This is our divine appointment from God in the generation in which we live. We won't have to force it. We will flow with it as God pours out his Spirit in this hour of restoration to reach the world.

Will you be one of the people at the end of the age who will dare to believe God's word concerning the supernatural? Will you make each day a masterpiece for God by living in a state of expectancy that he will channel his power in and through you? Most important of all, will you decide to pay the price for wielding the supernatural power of God? This is the divine appointment held out to us: move in the miraculous!

EIGHT

Paying the Price

HEALING. Prophecy. Word of knowledge. Miracles. All these and more are meant to be part of the church's arsenal as it confronts the world, the flesh, and the devil in the name of Jesus Christ. That means they are to be operative in the lives of each one of us who are soldiers in God's army. But how do we go about making them more a part of our personal Christian experience?

Consistent operation of the gifts of the Spirit is for the passionate, not the passive. God tells us to "eagerly desire spiritual gifts" (1 Cor 14:1); the Greek expression here rendered "eagerly seek" could also be translated "covet earnestly; to have warmth of feeling for." This is one area where Scripture instructs us to be white-hot in our pursuit of God.

Considering the urgency of the hour and the depth of people's need, how could we be anything *but* passionate in our pursuit of God? Our motivation is not to gain personal prominence in a "signs and wonders ministry" but to see the church of Jesus Christ fulfill its commission to "proclaim freedom for the prisoners and recovery of sight for the blind, to release the oppressed, to proclaim the year of the Lord's favor" (Lk 4:18-19).

There are no shortcuts to moving in the miraculous. Minimum dedication cannot lead to maximum blessing! It is true that everything in the Christian experience comes to us unmerited, by God's grace. Yet Scripture also indicates that we will find the riches of God to the degree that we pursue them. "He rewards those who *earnestly* seek him" (Heb 11:6).

If we are going to experience the miracle-working power of God surging through our lives and service, we must decide to pay the price. Here are some essential steps to moving in the miraculous.

Spend Time in God's Presence Consistently

The psalmist says that "Those who seek the Lord lack no good thing" (Ps 34:10). "Those who know their God," promises Daniel, "shall be strong and do exploits" (Dn 11:32). Doing exploits of faith requires vital, vibrant communion with God on a regular basis.

We need to know God intimately, so that our faith rests not on a formula but in a God who is himself faithful: "the same yesterday and today and forever" (Heb 13:8). This kind of faith is the result of a strong relationship nurtured by prayer.

The book of Acts describes how the good news penetrated the then-known world. The gospel as it was proclaimed was attested by signs and wonders. How does it begin? With the disciples gathered in the upper room for prayer.

I have also found it interesting to note that Acts is addressed to "Theophilus," which means "one who loves God," rather than to "Theologius," or "one who studies God." Not that scholarship and personal Scripture study are wrong. But the emphasis must be on growing in intimacy with God, not just growing in intellectual knowledge about him.

This matter of consistent time in God's presence is so important that I will devote two entire chapters to it. For now, it is enough simply to note that it is one of the basic steps to moving in the miraculous.

Cultivate a Sensitivity to the Holy Spirit

"Those who are led by the Spirit of God are sons of God," Paul says (Rom 8:14). We could turn this sentence around and say "those who are sons and daughters of God will be led by the Spirit of God." The Holy Spirit is a person, not an "it" or some kind of "force." Because he is a person, we can have a relationship with him. And, as in any relationship, there will be communication between us. We are to be guided and directed by the inner promptings of the Spirit.

Learning to recognize these inner promptings is a skill to be developed. Remember Elijah? How did he know to ignore the fire and the flood and the earthquake and listen for the "still, small voice" (see 1 Kgs 19:12)? Because he had heard that voice before. He knew what it sounded like. He knew when he was hearing it—and when he wasn't. Our goal is to reach this same level of sensitivity and confidence in being led by the Spirit. Here are some key ingredients:

—Regularly set aside times of solitude, to still your spirit and "clear the channels" so that you can hear God speak to you.

—Take necessary steps to block out interruptions and distractions.

—Reflect on the goodness of God and acknowledge his presence.

—Ask the Holy Spirit to help you hear him: "I love you, Holy Spirit. I depend on your guidance. Attune me to the sound of your voice."

—*Obey* the promptings you receive. "Do whatever he tells you" (Jn 2:5). Don't forget to seek counsel and confirmation from other believers when this involves something major.

—Don't grieve the Spirit by rebellious conduct (see Eph 4:30).

Live a Life of Righteousness, Purity, and Holiness

"The eyes of the Lord run to and fro throughout the whole earth in order to show himself strong on behalf of those whose hearts are blameless towards him" (2 Chr 16:9).

If we want to see the power of God flow through us, we must uphold the purity of God within us. If we sincerely want to move in the miraculous, we must renounce all wrongdoing and resolve to obey the Spirit's promptings in every area of life. If God is speaking to you about bitterness, unforgiveness, sinful anger, or jealousy, repent and forsake it today. The same holds for any movies, videos, magazines, clothes, or companions that displease God and contradict his word. Heed his voice! Don't compromise. Don't let doublemindedness short-circuit a full release of the Spirit in your life. As you faithfully root out areas of sin and clarify questionable "gray areas" by the Spirit's guidance, you will experience the power of God with ever greater intensity.

Pray for and Cultivate Boldness and Persistence

Many Christians don't realize that God expects us to pray for boldness as well as for signs and wonders in our Christian life. Look at the early church:

> Now, Lord, consider their threats and enable your servants to speak your word with great boldness. Stretch out your hand to heal and perform miraculous signs and wonders through the name of your holy servant Jesus. (Acts 4:29-30)

We need to pray for boldness, for Christ-confidence, so that we can live out our convictions in a manner that carries authority and is not timid. We must be willing to be "fools for Christ," stepping out in Spirit-led reckless abandon and acting on our faith. Consider the blind man, Bartimaeus, and how in the midst of a crowd he uninhibitedly shouted out, "Have mercy on me! Have mercy on me!" (see Mk 10:46-53).

Never let embarrassment keep you from the will of God. "For God did not give us a spirit of timidity, but a spirit of power, of love and of self-discipline" (2 Tm 1:7). Seize opportunities to pray for the sick. Capitalize on times when you can watch others moving in the healing ministries or the gifts of the Spirit. Ask others who have been used mightily in God's service to pray over you.

In addition, never let apparent failures and setbacks keep you from the will of God. "The righteous man falls seven times but rises again" (Prv 24:16). As an individual learning to step out in the miraculous, *be radically committed to persistence.*

David Livingstone, Christian "hall-of-famer" from another era, once said: "I determined never to stop until I have come to the end and achieved my purpose. By unfaltering persistence and faith in God, I will conquer."

Remember, the race is not always won by the swift. Sometimes it is won by those who simply keep on running!

Years back there was an eighteen-year-old freshman in Bible college who was very undisciplined and desirous of one day becoming a professional baseball player. As a youth he shook hands with Babe Ruth who told him, "Hey, you're big enough to make a good first baseman."

Although he was too poor to afford a ring, he got engaged to a girl named Emily. At a May Class Night he bought her a fifty-cent corsage but discovered she wouldn't wear it. She told him the engagement was off and she was going to marry another, someone more stable, a senior. When this happened the young man felt like giving up. "All the stars seemed to fall out of the sky," he said.

Later a fellow came over and reminded him of the scriptural truth that God is "the God of all encouragement." The Lord used this to jolt him into reality concerning his state. He decided not to give up but to be serious about seizing his destiny and fulfilling his ministry. He determined not to get side-tracked in his mission for God. He would persist until he achieved what God truly had called him to do.

Today he is one of the most respected and admired men of God in the entire world. He's a friend of presidents and world leaders. He has led more people to Christ than perhaps any man in history. His name? Billy Graham.

Dwight L. Moody held one of his early crusades in Chicago with three thousand present. For some strange reason he decided to postpone his "invitation to follow

Christ" and told the people, "Come tomorrow night." Subsequently, the Great Chicago Fire broke out in which scores were killed and thousands of buildings were destroyed in the holocaust. Dwight knew he had blundered terribly and was tempted to wallow in self-pity and condemnation. But he too was a man of godly persistence. He got up, learned from his mistake, and eventually won millions to Jesus Christ through his decades-long ministry.

Champions don't give up, they get up! "Nothing in the world can take the place of persistence. Talent will not—nothing is more common than unsuccessful men with talent. Genius will not—unrewarded genius is almost a proverb. Education will not—the world is full of educated derelicts. Persistence and determination are all powerful" (Calvin Coolidge).

Build Your Faith by Meditating on God's Word

"If you remain in me and my words remain in you," Jesus promised, "ask whatever you wish, and it will be given you" (Jn 15:7).

What a stupendous promise! But note the condition: "*If* my words remain in you. . . ." Whether it is moving in the miraculous or any other godly desire, the Lord promises us success if we will meet this condition (see Josh 1:8; Ps 1:1-3). There simply is no substitute for regular meditation on God's word.

Solid grounding in God's word also protects us from presumption, as we wait on him to illuminate the Scripture and take us beyond head-knowledge to heart-knowledge.

"Without faith it is impossible to please God" (Heb 11:6). Note that the writer does not say "without prayer," or "without giving money," but "without *faith.*" Faith is the key to growing in God.

How does faith come? By exposure to the word of God in

concert with the Holy Spirit (see Rom 10:17). So let's make up our minds to soak ourselves in the Scriptures.

Once there was a little girl whose mother told her to go outside and pick peaches. It was very hot outside, and picking peaches wasn't much fun. Day after day she faithfully labored at her task, struggling through the heat and discomfort. Months later, when the little girl sat down to breakfast one cold winter morning, her mother served her a slice of toast with some delicious peach preserve on top. Now the little girl felt different about those hot days spent picking peaches. It had taken time, but she was now enjoying the fruit of her labors.

That's how it sometimes is with us and our meditation on Scripture. It's dry; we seem to be getting nothing out of it. But later, under the illumination of God's Spirit, it comes alive in our experience. We derive the benefit if we remain steadfast.

To build your faith for moving in the miraculous, meditate on Scriptures pertaining to the greatness of God, faith, healing, boldness, and so on. Memorizing such passages is very helpful. Personalizing them—restating them as personal affirmations, rather than simply as universal principles—can release even greater faith. A few years ago I wrote a small tract called "Biblical Confessions to Build Your Faith." It brings together some faith-building scriptural truths in a form in which they can be stated aloud as personal affirmations. Here are some excerpts from that tract, to help get you started. Refer to it often and watch your faith grow!

I'm not just an ordinary man or woman; I am a son or daughter of the living God. I'm not just another person; I am an heir of God and a joint heir with Jesus Christ. I'm not just an old sinner; I am a new creation in Jesus, my Lord. I am part of a chosen generation, a royal priesthood, a holy nation; I am one of God's people.

I'm not under guilt or condemnation. There is no condemnation for those in Christ Jesus. Satan is a liar. I will not listen to his accusations. No weapon formed against me will prosper. I will confute every tongue rising against me in judgment.

*

My mind is being renewed by the word of God. I pull down strongholds, I cast down imaginings, I bring every thought captive to the obedience of Christ.

*

I am accepted in the Beloved. If God be for me, who can be against me? Nothing can separate me from the love of Christ.

*

I am not a slave to sin. I am a slave of God and a slave of righteousness. I have been delivered out of the kingdom of darkness. I'm now part of the kingdom of God. I don't have to serve sin anymore. Sin no longer has dominion over me.

*

Satan is defeated: the Son of God came into the world to destroy the works of the devil. No longer will he oppress me. I defeat him by the blood of the Lamb, by the word of my testimony, loving not my life even unto death. I submit to God; I resist the devil and he will flee from me.

*

No temptation will overtake me that is not common to man. God is faithful; he will not let me be tempted beyond my strength but with the temptation will also provide a way of escape that I may be able to endure it.

*

I will stand fast in the liberty with which Christ has made me free. Where the Spirit of the Lord is, there is liberty. The law of the Spirit of life in Jesus Christ has set me free from the law of sin and death.

I will reign as a king in life through Jesus Christ. I am strong; the word of God abides in me; and I have overcome the evil one. I am more than a conqueror through Christ who loves me. I am an overcomer. I can do all things in Christ who strengthens me. Thanks be to God who gives me the victory through Jesus Christ, my Lord!

*

I give no place to fear in my life. That which a man fears comes upon him. The fear of man brings a snare, but perfect love casts out fear. I sought the Lord and he heard me and delivered me from all my fears.

*

The Lord is my light and my salvation; whom shall I fear? The Lord is the strength of my life; of whom shall I be afraid? God is my refuge and strength, a very present help in trouble. Therefore I will not fear.

*

If I were still trying to please men, I should not be a servant of Jesus Christ. But I am a servant of the most high God. I fear not, for he is with me. I shall not be dismayed, for he is my God. He will strengthen me, he will help me, he will uphold me with his victorious right hand. I am not ashamed of the gospel, for it is the power of God unto salvation to those who believe.

*

I am a minister of reconciliation. I am an ambassador for Jesus Christ. I received power when the Holy Spirit came upon me to be his witness. His word never returns void but always accomplishes the purpose for which he sent it.

*

I am righteous; therefore I am bold as a lion. He will never fail me nor forsake me; therefore I can boldly say, The Lord is my helper, I shall not be afraid. What can man do to me?

Lord, grant to your servant to speak your word with all boldness while you stretch out your hand to heal, and signs and wonders are performed through the name of your holy servant Jesus!

*

All things are possible to him who believes. If I have faith as a grain of mustard seed, I can say to a mountain, "Move!" and it will move, and nothing will be impossible to me.

*

I am a believer, not a doubter. I have faith towards God. My faith is not in myself or in the realm of my feelings but in a living God who will never fail me nor forsake me. I walk by faith and not by sight.

*

One thing I do: forgetting what lies behind and straining forward to what lies ahead, I press on toward the goal for the prize of the upward call of God in Christ Jesus, my Lord. I put my hand to the plow and I do not look back. I run to win.

*

Jesus ever lives to make intercession for me. He is able to do far more abundantly than I can ask or think. He who began a good work in me will bring it to completion at the day of Christ Jesus.

*

I will be anxious for nothing. He will keep me in perfect peace, for my mind is stayed on him.

*

I have been crucified with Christ; nevertheless I live. And the life I now live, I live by faith in the Son of God, who loved me and gave himself for me. I choose this day to live by faith, to walk by faith, to see with eyes of faith. I will go from faith to faith, from strength to strength, from glory to glory!

*

I look not to healing but to the Healer: Jesus Christ, my Lord. My body is for the Lord and the Lord is for my body. He bore away my sicknesses and carried away my diseases. By his stripes I am healed. The same Spirit that raised Jesus from the dead is at work in my mortal body, giving me life.

*

I am not lukewarm. I am not a compromiser. I will not be conformed to this world. I am a partaker of his divine nature. God indwells my body. His grace is sufficient for me, and his power is made perfect in my weakness.

*

I am not weighed down by the cares of this life. I cast my cares upon the Lord.

*

Whatever the task this day, I will do it heartily, as serving the Lord.

*

The Spirit of the Lord is upon me. He has anointed me to preach good news to the poor. He has sent me to proclaim release to the captives, recovery of sight to the blind, to set at liberty those who are oppressed, to bind up the broken-hearted, and to proclaim the acceptable year of the Lord.

*

When the enemy comes in like a flood, the Spirit of the Lord will raise up a standard. I am a part of that standard. I am a soldier in the army of salvation that God is raising up to save this world.

*

I am part of the end-times visitation of the Spirit. Therefore I have a sense of destiny.

*

I will not despise the day of small beginnings. The vision awaits its time; it hastens to the end; it will not fail. If it seem slow, I shall wait for it. It will surely come. It will not delay.

*

Jesus is restoring his church. He is coming back for a

glorious church without spot or wrinkle or blemish or any such thing. It will be a triumphant church. It will kick in the gates of hell.

*

I am a pioneer, not a settler. I am on the front lines. I have counted the cost. I will pay the price. I am giving my utmost for his highest. I press on toward the goal for the prize of the high call of God in Christ Jesus, my Lord. I am out to change my generation. I am beginning *today*.

These, then, are some steps we can take to believe God and experience the fullness of his supernatural power in our lives.

Will you join me in this exciting hour of church restoration as God fashions a people who refuse to limit the Holy One of Israel? Will you fulfill your divine appointment to move in the miraculous?

Summon your power, O God;
   show us your strength, O God,
   as you have done before. (Ps 68:28)

Part IV

Divine Appointment *with* God: Praying in His Presence

May he be enthroned in God's presence forever; appoint your love and faithfulness to protect him. (Ps 61:7)

NINE

Pressure, Prayer, and Providence

THERE'S SOMETHING ABOUT A TELEPHONE ringing at 6:30 in the morning. Somehow you just know it's not going to be good news.

On this particular morning, the voice on the other end of the line was that of my mother-in-law. It sounded a bit strained.

"Larry, this is Mom. Have you seen this morning's paper yet?"

"Uhhhhhh...no." I hadn't yet shaken the cobwebs from my still half-asleep brain. But something was obviously wrong. I wondered what it might be this time. Did someone important die? Was there an assassination?

"Well, there's an article in this morning's *Washington Post* that says someone is suing you."

"What?" I said. "Suing? Who? I mean, who's suing me? What for?"

"The author of some book on psychology." Mom skimmed hurriedly through the article. "He says you spread inaccurate information about him, you and some other Christian leaders. Larry, it says he's suing all of you for over twenty million dollars!"

"Twenty million dollars!" I gasped. I was certainly wide awake

now. What on earth could be happening? It felt like a crazy dream.

"Maybe it's just a publicity stunt," Mom suggested. There was hope but not much conviction in her voice.

I hung up, burst out of bed, and hauled the morning paper in from the front porch. There was the story, all right. Doris and I read it through several times. My brain felt numb and my stomach was churning. Back in high school, when the baseball team won a big game, it was a thrill to see my name in the newspaper. This was no thrill.

"Doris," I finally said. "We've got to pray. I mean *really* pray."

We clasped hands and dropped to our knees. It was all I could do to speak coherently amid the storm of emotion I was experiencing.

"Lord God," I began. "Lord . . . I don't know what this is all about. If I've done something wrong, I'll do whatever your word tells me to do to make it right. I'm keeping my eyes fixed on you, Lord. Help me to be steadfast in trusting you to deliver me."

Doris and I ended our prayer by claiming Jesus' promise recorded in Mark 11:24: "Whatever you ask for in prayer, believe that you have received it, and it will be yours."

That morning in 1980 marked the beginning of an ordeal that lasted four years and gave me a complete education in the need for, and the effectiveness of, persistent prayer. I had cast my lot with God. Now I would have to remain steadfast and obedient, resisting fear and calling on the name of the Lord for victory. "He will have no fear of bad news; his heart is steadfast, trusting in the Lord. His heart is secure, he will have no fear; in the end he will look in triumph on his foes" (Ps 112:7-8).

What was the lawsuit all about?

About a year earlier, a report had been circulating, both in the United States and abroad, that the author of a best-selling pop-psychology book had taken his own life.

The first time I heard the report was at a large Christian conference. Naturally, I was curious and wanted to verify it. After all, the book in question had to do with how to be happy and fulfilled. For the author of such a book to commit suicide would be a striking contradiction and a powerful lesson on the inadequacy of seeking peace apart from Jesus Christ.

I had lunch with the speaker who had made the comment, a respected teacher on family life, and asked him about what he had said. He told me he had heard the report from another man internationally known in Christian ministry. It appeared that the sad and shocking story was indeed true, or so I thought.

Several months later I repeated the erroneous information during a speaking engagement in California. Word eventually got back to the author, who lived nearby. To borrow a phrase from Mark Twain, it seemed that the reports of his death were "greatly exaggerated." He was still very much alive. Actually, I had never mentioned the man's name—in fact, at that point I didn't even *know* his name. I had simply referred to him as "the author of. . . ." But as a practical matter, it amounted to pretty much the same thing.

I could certainly understand why the man was upset. A false report like the one I had unwittingly spread was indeed damaging to his reputation. I felt horrible about the whole thing. I knew I had not acted maliciously, but the damage had been done. The question now was what I could do to set matters right.

The New Testament offers some pretty clear prescriptions for resolving relationship problems: "If you are offering your gift at the altar and there remember that your brother has something against you, leave your gift there in front of the altar. First go and be reconciled to your brother; then come and offer your gift" (Mt 5:23-24). "If your brother sins against you, go and show him his fault, just between the two of you. If he listens to you, you have won your brother over" (Mt 18:15).

The biblical course of action seemed clear. I should relate to the man whose reputation I had unintentionally harmed as my brother (I had been told he was a church member). Obviously he "had something against me"; I should take it upon myself to pursue reconciliation and should consider it an extremely high priority. I should try to resolve matters "just between the two of us," ask for forgiveness, and try to "win my brother over."

I tried everything I could think of. I wrote him a letter asking his forgiveness. I phoned him at home three times and asked him to forgive me. But it was all to no avail. His attorneys advised him not to communicate with me outside legal channels. My attorneys, who were Christians and understood why I was seeking reconciliation, advised me not to fly across the country and go directly to his door, which I considered doing several times, lest it be construed as harassment.

So there was nothing to do but follow through the legal process and persist in prayer. The next four years were a nightmare of complex courtroom maneuvers, grueling days of giving depositions, rapidly growing legal fees, and endless nights battling thoughts like, "It's all over . . . I'm going to lose everything . . . the church will be devastated . . . my ministry is finished . . . I'm ruined for life."

The pressure would have been unbearable had it not been for the grace of God poured out through fervent and consistent prayer and for the unwavering support of brothers and sisters in Christ. The story was covered in the leading Christian magazines, and innumerable Christians prayed, fasted, and supported me with notes of encouragement and contributions to a legal defense fund.

Closer to home, I was sustained by loyal friends in the Christian community to which we belong. Chip Ward, a fellow leader in the church, came over immediately upon hearing news of the lawsuit and offered to sell his house if it would help cover legal expenses. Charles Mahaney, my friend and co-laborer in the ministry for more than twelve years, unfailingly provided a listening ear and many words of encouragement. And there were many others, like Steve Shank, Bill Galbraith, Ché Ahn, Chuck Thompson, Dick Moore, Brent Detwiler, and Rob Robison, who gave meaning to the proverb, "A friend loves at all times, and a brother is born for adversity" (Prv 17:17).

And, of course, there was Doris. "A wife of noble character who can find? She is worth far more than rubies. Her husband has full confidence in her and lacks nothing of value" (Prv 31:10-11). Her prayers and encouragement enabled me to "keep the faith" and trust God for victory throughout the entire ordeal.

During this time, J. Oswald Sanders' poem about the making of a man of God became very real to me:

When God wants to drill a man
   and thrill a man
   and skill a man,
When God wants to mold a man
   to play the noblest part;
When he yearns with all his heart
   to create so great and bold a man
That all the world shall be amazed,
Watch his methods, watch his ways!
How he ruthlessly perfects
   whom he royally elects!
How he hammers him and hurts him,
   and with mighty blows converts him
Into trial shapes of clay which
   only God understands;
While his tortured heart is crying
   and he lifts beseeching hands!
How he bends but never breaks
   when his good he undertakes;
How he uses whom he chooses
   and with every purpose fuses him;

by every act induces him
To try his splendor out—
God knows what he's about!
     (from *Spiritual Leadership,* Moody Press, 1967)

Finally, after four years of praying persistently for God's intervention, the day of decision arrived. My attorneys had appealed to the judge to adjust a previous ruling we felt had unfairly undermined my case. If the judge agreed to our request, the opposition's strategy would be blocked and the case would, for all practical purposes, be over.

As I stood in the stark, cold courtroom, hanging on to every word uttered by the judge and the attorneys, I called to mind the Scripture, "The king's heart is in the hand of the Lord; he directs it like a watercourse wherever he pleases" (Prv 21:1). Did that Scripture apply to judges as well as to kings?

"My instinct," the judge began slowly, "tells me I should grant this in favor of Mr. Tomczak."

It was all over. The judge's heart was turned. I almost did a backflip right there in the courtroom!

Later that day, as my attorneys had anticipated, the opposition agreed to settle the case. We agreed on a small financial settlement, which I considered fair and was glad to pay. The three of us who had been named in the suit heaved a sigh of relief, shed a few tears of thanksgiving, and went home.

Not only had I just completed a lesson on our legal system that I would never forget, I also learned a lot about what Jesus meant when he said that we "should always pray and not give up" (Lk 18:1). When we are under pressure, when the heat is on, there is nothing like prayer to pull us through.

But there is another aspect to prayer, one we might lose sight of if we were to talk about prayer only in the context of coping with adversity. Scripture says we should *always* pray, not pray just when the chips are down. Prayer is an expression of a living, growing relationship with our heavenly Father. It should be a constant factor in our lives, an abiding characteristic, not something we resort to *only* when times are tough.

The greatest example of this in my own life was my father. I had the joy of leading Dad into a deeper relationship with Christ when he was sixty-two years of age. From then until the day he died, Dad was first and foremost a man of childlike faith and persevering prayer.

Dad prayed believing that his only daughter would find a Christian husband before his death, even though she was already in her mid-thirties and had no apparent "prospects" on the horizon. His prayers were answered through a divine appointment when God caused my sister to cross paths with a Christian leader from Canada. You can imagine the special joy Dad took in "giving away the bride" at their wedding.

Dad once prayed believing that God would open the door for him to visit with a cancer-stricken friend in a hospital ward where visitors were not normally allowed. Through a series of apparent coincidences, Dad was able to slip into his friend's room and lead him to the Lord just before he died.

Dad prayed believing for a peaceful departure from this life, devoid of prolonged illness or suffering. By God's mercy, his homecoming took place on a Sunday morning, just after returning from our worship service, as he settled down on the couch for his daily personal Scripture meditation. That day, the heading atop the page was "Prayer." He started reading, bowed his head, and went home! As someone has said, "A sudden, peaceful death is the kiss of God upon one's soul."

I miss Dad, though it is a joy to know he is with the Lord. The very day Dad's notice appeared in the obituaries, someone showed me a statement made by the famous evangelist Dwight L. Moody:

Some day you will read in the papers that D.L. Moody of East Northfield is dead. Don't you believe a word of it! At that moment I shall be more alive than I am now. I shall have gone up higher, that is all—out of this old clay body into one that is immortal; a body that death cannot touch, the sun cannot taint, a body fashioned after his glorious body.

Dad left behind the legacy of a life dedicated to serving God and God's people. Dad prayed. Dad believed. His example lives on even through the pages of this book, calling you and me to faithfully fulfill our daily divine appointment with God, to consistent and life-giving prayer. In the aftermath of Dad's death, I reviewed the many Scriptures that speak to us of the life to come, the life that awaits us when this earthly life is over. I was repeatedly struck by how many of the glories of eternal life actually come to us even now as we participate in the life of heaven through prayer.

The psalmist spoke of the exaltation of being "enthroned in God's presence forever" (Ps 61:7). A foretaste of that exaltation can be ours now, as we place ourselves in God's presence day by day.

David said, "You have made known to me the path of life; you will fill me with joy in your presence, with eternal pleasures at your right hand" (Ps 16:11). That same providential guidance, that same joy, that same unending bliss, can be ours now as we open our hearts to God in prayer.

May we learn more and more how to enter into the life that God makes available to us in prayer! May we make our own the prayer of Moses: "Moses said to the Lord, 'You have said, "I know you by name and you have found favor with me." If I have found favor in your eyes, teach me your ways so I may know you and continue to find favor with you'" (Ex 33:12-13).

Learning the ways of prayer, through a daily divine appointment in his presence, will be our task in the next chapter.

TEN

Developing Consistency in Prayer

S OMETIMES THE ODDEST THINGS happen when we pray.
More than ten years ago, before I was even married, I heard the Lord tell me during prayer that he wanted me to adopt a child some day.

I certainly wanted to have children of my own, but I sensed God planting a "seed thought" in my spirit about adoption. This thought lined up with a number of convictions I held. I was deeply grieved about the number of supposedly un-wanted children slaughtered by abortion, and I recognized adoption as one solution to the total problem. I also wanted to live out the kind of faith James talked about: "Religion that God our Father accepts as pure and faultless is this: to look after orphans and widows in their distress" (Jas 1:27).

Obviously, there was no way this prompting could be fulfilled right away. But I knew it was more than just a "nice idea." It was a word of God, and its fulfillment was only a matter of time. Like Mary, I "treasured up all these things and pondered them in my heart" (see Lk 2:19).

The sense returning from time to time over the next several years was God's way of reminding me about it. Then, after seven delightful years of marriage and three natural children, it came back to stay. Doris and I both had a strong stirring that the time had come. And, as we sought the Lord earnestly in our personal prayer, a more developed sense of guidance emerged: we were to adopt a foreign child, a girl, about three years of age.

The pieces began falling in place rapidly. God had already been at work behind the scenes, preparing in advance the good work that we were called to do (see Eph 2:10). I was scheduled to visit Seoul, Korea, in just three months. That seemed less than completely coincidental. Then I learned that a close friend of mine was in touch with a woman who assisted in expediting adoptions from Korea. Finally, one of the three men who was to accompany me on the trip, himself of Korean descent, had an uncle in Korea who knew the director of an orphanage in Seoul. By now it seemed clear that my upcoming trip was to include a remarkable divine appointment with my own future daughter!

I visited several children's homes in Seoul, waiting to see how God would unfold his plan. At one point I was interviewed by the director of a particular child welfare agency, to be approved as a prospective adoptive parent. As our interview ended, we got up and walked toward a door at one end of his office. Just then someone opened the door and I could see, at the far end of the adjoining room, a woman holding a little Korean girl. The girl appeared to be about three years old.

She's the one. I sensed God speaking to my spirit as clearly as if he had spoken in an audible voice. *She's the one I told you about. That's your new daughter.*

Everything was arranged with remarkable speed. Six months later my wife and I, our three little ones, and my father and mother greeted our new family member at the airport. A Korean woman from a nearby church, returning from a visit to Seoul, had escorted our little girl home. In the meantime, the Lord had given us the perfect name for our new daughter, who once had been abandoned on the streets of Seoul. Her name was Renee. In French it means "born again" or "given a second chance."

Renee's adoption is just a dramatic example of something that occurs frequently: God's plan being announced and implemented through the life of a believer whose spirit is tuned to God in prayer. A life of deep, abiding communion with God is the indispensable prerequisite for being led by his Spirit.

Of course, very few of us really need to be persuaded that consistent personal prayer is a critical component of our Christian life.

We have all noticed how prominent prayer was in the life of Jesus, as reflected in such passages as Mark 1:35: "Very early in the morning, while it was still dark, Jesus got up, left the house and went off to a solitary place, where he prayed."

We have also noticed the importance of prayer in the life of the early church. The first disciples didn't ask Jesus to teach them to *preach*; they asked him to teach them to *pray* (see Lk 11:1). In the book of Acts, we find that the outpouring of the Holy Spirit on Pentecost and the subsequent ingathering of some 3,000 men and women, recorded in chapter two, came as a result of the fervent prayer and intercession recorded in chapter one.

And we have all heard pearls of wisdom about prayer uttered by great men and women of God throughout Christian history. John Wesley restated Philippians 4:6 to emphasize that "the Lord will do everything by prayer, and nothing without prayer." Jonathan Edwards, a pioneer of the Great Awakening, underlined the necessity of "extraordinary prayer" to usher in revival.

Agreeing that prayer is important is not our problem. Our problem is that when all is said and done, much is said and little is done! We have good intentions, but we fail to act on them. One of the speakers at a conference I attended told how he had earnestly pleaded with God to "help me become a man of prayer"—and was surprised to hear God chuckle in reply: "You don't really mean that, do you?" He realized he had been making that same request since boyhood, but he had never taken seriously the challenge to follow through on it.

How can we develop greater faithfulness and greater fruitfulness in prayer? Here are some practical suggestions that have been of help to me and to many others.

Call to Mind the Benefits of Prayer

In Psalm 103, the psalmist reminds himself to "Praise the Lord, O my soul; and forget not all his benefits" (Ps 103:2). That's a good reminder for us as well, especially in regard to prayer. I have written down a brief list of some of these benefits, to help me get motivated for prayer during periods of spiritual dryness. A consistent prayer life:

—Brings delight to the heart of God, our Father.

—Provides an opportunity for us to receive his daily instructions and his daily empowering to carry them out. The reason so many of us lack purpose and power in our lives is that we fail to connect ourselves to the source of purpose and power.

—Opens up dialogue with God in which we can "cast our cares upon him" (1 Pt 5:7).

—Provides spiritual cleansing from the world's contamination and "breaks up the fallow ground" of our hearts to keep them humble and pure before God.

—Brings us into spiritual warfare, so that we can break the power of the enemy in our own life, in our family, in the church, and in the world.

—Cultivates in us a greater sensitivity to the leadings of the Holy Spirit, as we have seen in the story of Renee's adoption.

—Sharpens our discernment of the workings of evil spirits.

Make Prayer a Priority

A consistent prayer life doesn't "just happen." We have to *make* it happen. And we will never simply "find time" for prayer; we will have to make time for it. Our conviction about the importance of prayer must be translated into action by reordering our use of time and energy accordingly.

It's a constant struggle, even for the most accomplished "pray-ers." On the trip to Korea I have already mentioned, I learned a great deal about prayer and church growth from Dr. Paul Yonggi Cho, pastor of the Full Gospel Church, the world's largest church, having more than half a million members. Dr. Cho credits the amazing growth of his church primarily to an emphasis on prayer and intercession. He humbly admits that daily prayer for him is still a battle with fleshly tendencies and distraction. That testimony encouraged me concerning my own struggles in the area but also spurred me to redouble my efforts to overcome them.

Be Motivated by Grace, Not by Legalism

As we set about the task of developing consistency in our prayer life, it is important that we resist the snare of legalism. Many Christians, in their quest for greater discipline in prayer, unconsciously slip into trying to establish their righteousness through works of the flesh. They begin to think that if they just get up a little earlier in the morning or spend just a few more minutes on their knees, God will be more pleased with them. They seem to picture God sitting up in heaven with a cosmic clipboard in his hands, checking off who has completed a daily prayer time and who has slipped up.

Godly discipline is necessary, of course. Prayer does not come naturally; it comes supernaturally. We are called to cooperate with the Holy Spirit in bearing the fruit of self-control in our lives. We have to invest some effort and apply some discipline to ourselves.

But we must be on guard against any motivation to pray that seeks to establish our own position before God. Rather, we should begin by acknowledging the position that Jesus has won for us and rest secure in God's unconditional acceptance of us. Then we can view prayer not as a "have-to" but as a "get-to." Progress will come, not by gritting our teeth and mustering up more willpower but by yielding to God's Spirit and with his help "exercising ourselves unto godliness" (see 1 Tm 4:7).

Early to Bed, Early to Rise . . .

"In vain you rise early and stay up late" (Ps 127:2). I think the psalmist actually had something a little bit different in mind when he wrote these lines, but his words do remind us of a simple fact: you can't stay up late at night and then expect to be able to wake up bright and early and ready to pray.

This is elementary. But it is amazing how many Christians overlook it. They sit up until the small hours of the morning, having fellowship with Ted Koppel, Johnny Carson, and David Letterman, then wonder why they miss their devotional time because they can't seem to get out of bed in the morning.

Nowhere, of course, does the Bible command, "Thou shalt get up early to pray." But even if it is not specifically commanded, it is at least strongly endorsed. Consider the following.

King David: "Morning by morning, O Lord, you hear my voice; morning by morning I lay my requests before you and wait in expectation" (Ps 5:3).

Elkanah and Hannah, parents of the prophet Samuel: "Early the next morning they arose and worshiped before the Lord" (1 Sm 1:19).

Hezekiah: "Early the next morning King Hezekiah gathered the city officials together and went up to the temple of the Lord" (2 Chr 29:20).

Jesus: "Very early in the morning, while it was still dark, Jesus got up, left the house and went off to a solitary place, where he prayed" (Mk 1:35).

I am sure there are people who have very regular and very profitable prayer times during other parts of the day. But long experience tells me that for most of us, early morning is the best—and perhaps the only—reliable time slot available, especially for anyone who has little ones running around the house. That's when our daily divine appointment is going to have to be scheduled. And if we are going to be serious about keeping it, we are going to have to arrange our evening schedules accordingly.

Find a Prayer Closet

Jesus specifically teaches us, "When you pray, go into your room, close the door and pray to your Father, who is unseen" (Mt 6:6). Again, he is speaking primarily about not being ostentatious in our prayer, showing off our piety before others. But there is a nugget of practical wisdom in his words as well. We have already seen how Jesus made it a regular practice to "go off to a solitary place" in order to spend time in prayer. The important point is to block out distractions. Have you ever noticed how hard it is to keep random thoughts from interfering with your prayer? Much of this is simple human nature. But there is also a spiritual component to it. Satan is definitely interested in "jamming the signals" when we are trying to communicate with God.

Mental discipline, then, is hard enough under the best of circumstances. We should make the task as easy as we can by seeing to it that distractions from outside sources are minimized when we pray. Find a place where the phone won't ring, where the children won't be milling about, where co-workers won't be knocking on the door, and where papers and other items won't draw your attention to mundane concerns.

It can be a corner of the basement, an attic, an unused room or office, even a closet. Look upon it as your special place set apart for prayer. Eventually you will develop a mental association between that place and the act of prayer, so that when you are there, praying will seem like the "natural" thing to do.

Develop a Personal Prayer Pattern

Each of us is unique. Therefore, each of us has a unique relationship with God and will normally develop our own unique way of praying to him. Moreover, God is the God of newness, of freshness, of change. We can expect the ways of prayer to be "new every morning."

But it is also important for us to give some structure to our prayer. Too much spontaneity does us more harm than good; it can leave us aimless and open to distraction. I recommend developing a simple, flexible pattern to follow during your prayer time. You needn't be rigid or mechanical with it; rather, you can look at it as a basic framework within which to be spontaneous. Each of us needs a pattern that is uniquely "our own," but I am convinced that each of us does need a pattern. Here, to give you one example, is mine.

The psalmist tells us to "enter his gates with thanksgiving" (Ps 100:4). After asking the Holy Spirit to "search my heart" for any unconfessed sin, I usually begin my time of prayer by thanking the Lord for all the things he has done in me, for me, and through me during the past twenty-four to forty-eight hours. This helps me approach the rest of my prayer time with an "attitude of gratitude."

"Yet a time is coming and has now come when the true worshipers will worship the Father in spirit and truth" (John 4:23). After thanksgiving, I usually flow into a time of reflective worship, meditating on the goodness and greatness of God.

Of course, if we are to reflect on God's attributes, we must know what they are and be able to put them into words. Perhaps this listing of the "ABC's" of God will prove helpful to you both for quiet meditation and for vocal prayer.

ABC's of God's Attributes

A —Abba, Able, Alive, All-knowing, All-powerful, Almighty, Alpha, Altogether Lovely

B —Beautiful, Bright and Morning Star, Benign

C —Comforter, Creator, Compassionate, Covenant-keeping, Caring, Counselor

D —Delightful, Devoted, Diligent

E —Eternal, Everlasting, Everything, Exalted, Excellent

F —Faithful, Father, Fearless, Forgiving, Friend

G —Generous, Gentle, Giving, Glorious, Good, Gracious, Great

H —Holy, Honest, Honorable, Humble

I —Immaculate, Immortal, In Control, Inspiring, Irresistible

J —Jealous, Joyful, Judge, Justifier, Just

K —Keeper, Kind, King

L —Lamb of God, Living, Long-suffering, Lord, Lovely, Loving, Lowly in Heart

M—Magnificent, Majestic, Maker, Master, Meek, Merciful, Messiah, Mighty

N —Near, Noble

O —Omega, Omnipotent, Omniscient, One, Only True God, Orderly

P —Peaceful, Personal, Powerful, Praiseworthy, Protector, Provider, Pure

Q —Quiet

R —Radiant, Real, Reigning, Reliable, Responsive, Righteous, Rock of Salvation, Royal

S —Sanctifier, Savior, Servant, Shepherd, Slow to Anger,
    Sovereign, Sustainer
T —Tender, Triumphant, True, Trustworthy
U—Unchanging, Unlimited, Unparalleled
V —Victorious, Vigilant, Virtuous
W—Wise, Wonderful, Worthy
Y —You Are My Everything!
Z —Zealous

Following thanksgiving, praise, and worship, I usually begin my prayers of petition as Paul urged Timothy to do: by praying for our governing leaders (see 1 Tm 2:1-3). I then flow into intercessory prayer for my wife, my children, my family, my friends, and myself. I then pray for the churches with which I am involved: for the leaders, all the ministries, and for the people.

I conclude by praying for other needs that the Spirit impresses upon my heart and by thanking God that he has heard my prayers. It is here that I intercede for people who are lost and for specific needs of the day.

Set a Realistic Goal

Realistic goals are, first of all, concrete goals. We won't meet with much success if we merely say, "I want to start praying more." We need to make it concrete: so many minutes a day for so many days, and so on.

Realistic goals are, second, reachable goals. Richard Foster, in his book *Celebration of Discipline,* observes that "Someone who has never jogged before should not throw himself into a twenty-six-mile marathon." In the same way, we are not likely to be able to succeed at praying three hours a day if we haven't yet consistently prayed for fifteen minutes a day. By setting a goal that helps assure us of success, we build our confidence to press on to greater achievement.

Plan on Persistence

As someone has said, "Starting out is easy, sticking to it is hard." If we are going to become consistent in prayer, we are going to have to persevere. What matters is not that we launch out in a blaze of glory, but that we stick with it, day after day, week after week, month after month, year after year. We need to orient ourselves to the long haul, not the short run.

Remember the familiar passage where Jesus teaches us to ask, seek, and knock (Lk 11:9)? The original Greek actually means "Ask and keep on asking . . . seek and keep on seeking . . . knock and keep on knocking." The need for perseverance is built into prayer.

Today, as God is moving to restore his church and evangelize the world, the Holy Spirit is issuing a renewed call to us to keep our daily divine appointment with God in prayer. We need not merely a mental assent to the priority of prayer but a Spirit-driven commitment to consistency in the practice of prayer.

May we rise up in response to this call! Like the widow Jesus cited, who gave the judge no rest until he heeded her plea (see Lk 18:1-8), may we too come persistently before our loving Father. As we do, may we see the heavens opened afresh, the Spirit poured out anew, the church restored, multitudes reached with the gospel, and the enemy crushed under our feet as we celebrate the return of our Lord Jesus Christ! "For Zion's sake I will not keep silent, for Jerusalem's sake I will not remain quiet, till her righteousness shines out like the dawn, her salvation like a blazing torch" (Is 62:1).

Part V

Our Divine Appointment: The Restoration of the Church to Reach the World

*Write down the revelation
and make it plain on tablets
so that a herald may run with it.
For the revelation awaits an appointed time;
it speaks of the end
and it will not prove false.
Though it linger, wait for it;
it will certainly come and will not delay.
(Hb 2:2-3)*

ELEVEN

What in the World Is Going On?

O NE EVENING, during a break from speaking at a conference, I took a relaxed stroll through a nearby neighborhood. The sounds of music and voices drew me to one particular area that had been cordoned off for a "block party." Most of the noise was coming from a set of massive speakers, blaring out rock music for a teen dance. The lyrics of one particular song caught my attention, soaring eerily through the strobe-lit evening air:

> Don't push me, 'cause I'm close to the edge;
> I'm tryin' not to lose my head.
> It's like a jungle sometimes; it makes me wonder
> How I keep from goin' under.
> ("The Message," by Grandmaster Flash)

Can you identify with the cry of the singer's heart? Can you hear the generation around us echoing his refrain?

Most of us are aware of what a rock poet told us years ago: "The times they are a-changin'." But do we realize just how serious and dramatic those changes really are? Understanding the present situation of the world and the church is crucial if we are to understand the divine appointment God has prepared for our generation.

We live in a time when centuries of Christian influence are being washed away. Christian values which shaped our lives for hundreds of years are eroding within the span of a single generation.

Things that were unthinkable twenty years ago are commonplace today. Twenty years ago, most people agreed that abortion was murder, that homosexuality was perversion, and that pornography was dehumanizing and exploitive of women. Not any more. Today's "enlightened" thinking says these are merely political issues, not moral ones, and that there are no moral absolutes. Even Dr. Benjamin Spock, whose *Baby and Child Care* guided millions of parents for decades, now says that living together before marriage can be good for older teenagers.

"I suppose there are sections of this country that have sunk as low as anything in history," Billy Graham has said. "No nation in history has ever been able to go in this direction and survive very long. I think the greatest threat to our nation is moral decadence."

In short, large segments of our population have simply lost the ability to tell right from wrong. Because they have rejected truth, their thinking has become futile. Modern society is not merely experiencing a temporary malfunction but a complete moral collapse. It is not just that the house has leaky plumbing and peeling wallpaper. Rather, its foundation has been blasted away, and the walls are starting to crumble. The situation in our day is painfully similar to that described by the apostle Paul when he described the downward spiral of rejecting truth, losing discernment, and finally floundering in moral chaos: "The wrath of God is being revealed from heaven against all the godlessness and wickedness of men who suppress the truth by their wickedness, since what may be known about God is plain to them, because God has made it plain to them. . . . For although they knew God, they neither glorified him as God nor gave thanks to him, but their thinking became futile and their foolish hearts were darkened. Although they claimed to be wise they became fools. . . . Therefore God gave them over in the sinful desires of their hearts to sexual impurity for the degrading of their bodies with one another . . . and received in themselves the due penalty for their perversion . . . . Furthermore, since they did not think it worthwhile to retain the knowledge of God, he gave them over to a depraved mind, to do what ought not to be done. They have become filled with every kind of wickedness, evil, greed and depravity. They are full of envy, murder, strife, deceit and malice. They are gossips, slanderers, God-haters, insolent, arrogant and boastful; they invent ways of doing evil; they disobey their parents; they are senseless, faithless, heartless, ruthless. Although they know God's righteous decree that those who do such things deserve death, they not only continue to do these very things but also approve of those who practice them" (Rom 1:18-19, 21-22, 24, 27-32).

The evidence of moral collapse surrounds us on every side:

Family. Divorce rates in the United States are now among the highest in the world. Eighteen million children live in what was once called "a broken home"; this figure is up 40 percent in just ten years. Yet the vast communications network of television, radio, movies, newspapers, and popular books and magazines continues to discredit biblical values concerning the family as outdated and restrictive of personal freedom.

Sexual Morality. Teenage pregnancies have increased by 33 percent in the past five years, despite the unprecedented availability of birth control and abortion. Twenty million people suffer from herpes and thousands now have contracted AIDS. Sexual abuse of children is increasing. Yet the multi-billion-dollar pornography industry flourishes under court protected "rights." Moreover, the media continually glamorize celebrities (whom young people tend to emulate) living in open sin. Adultery, fornication, and homosexuality are simply presented as normal expressions of "love."

Abortion. More than fifteen million unborn babies have been slaughtered in the womb since 1973: one every twenty seconds. The doctor, who needs parental permission to perform a tonsillectomy on a teenager, no longer needs it to perform an abortion on the same teenager. A major drug manufacturer is developing a do-it-yourself abortion suppository that will move abortions out of clinics and hospitals and into the privacy of your very own bathroom. Meanwhile, the National Organization for Women now bars opponents of legalized abortion from even speaking at their conferences. How's that for equal rights?

Youth Rebellion. God warned his people long ago: "It shall come to pass, if you will not harken unto the voice of the Lord thy God . . . . thy sons and thy daughters shall be taken into captivity" (Dt 28:15, 32). Today, parents find themselves increasingly unable to cope with youngsters being taken into captivity by drugs, destructive music, sexual immorality, and the occult.

Crime. In the United States today there is a murder every twenty-four minutes, a rape every seven minutes, a home burglary every ten seconds. But our ability to prevent crime or to apprehend those who commit it, and our willingness to punish those we do apprehend, is deteriorating.

Nuclear Terror. As more and more countries of the world become members of the "Nuclear Club," the chances multiply that one crazy action, or even one simple error in judgment, could start a chain reaction that would culminate in the destruction of most of the world.

In his classic study, *The Rise and Fall of the Roman Empire,* Edward Gibbon cites five main causes for the dissolution of that once-powerful civilization: collapse of the family; economic upheaval; obsession with sex and pleasure-seeking; emphasis on militarism; decay of religion from spiritual vitality to empty formality.

But will God's people be roused from slumber even as they see these same kinds of warning signs come to pass in modern

America and Europe? Although it may not be pleasant or popular, we must be brutally honest about the state of much of the Christian church today. The same confusion and compromise that prevail in society because of the rejection of truth are evident in many sectors of the church. For example:

—The United Methodist Church, the nation's second-largest Protestant denomination, has permitted avowed homosexuals to be ordained to the ministry.

—An Episcopal Cathedral in New York recently unveiled a statue called "The Christa"—a bronze female "Jesus," complete with bare breasts and rounded hips.

—The Presbyterian Church (U.S.A.) in its 195th General Assembly, issued a policy statement affirming the 1973 Supreme Court decision legalizing abortion and opposing "all measures which would serve to restrict full and equal access to contraception and abortion services to all women."

Small wonder that as large segments of the church make themselves indistinguishable from the world, their ability to impact the world wanes dramatically. When a major news magazine recently ranked the influence of thirty American professions and institutions, organized religion came in fourth from last.

What's the answer to the problems being faced by such broad segments of God's people? Clearly it is far too late in the game for superficial, cosmetic alterations or for a few new committees and programs. The problems run much deeper than that. So must the solutions. The words of Paul Kopp to a national convention of the American Baptist Church are worth noting:

We take the tired old horse, ribs showing, with little left on the bones, put on a brand new saddle, and mount the steed with new whip in hand. With a little beating and spurring, the old horse moves a few tired paces. Then we say, "There must be something wrong with the saddle and whip." New ones are brought forth and put on, and the same results occur. Too often, denominations are saddled and resaddled with new programs, with very little real spiritual progress . . . actually the need is for new spiritual power.

The sad state of the Christian churches really should come as no surprise to us. Hasn't God told us it would happen? "The Spirit *clearly says*," Paul reminded Timothy, "that in later times some will abandon the faith and follow deceiving [seducing] spirits" (1 Tm 4:1). In another letter, Paul told Timothy, "Mark this: There will be terrible times in the last days. People will be . . . lovers of pleasure rather than lovers of God—having a form of godliness but denying its power" (2 Tm 3:1, 5).

These passages don't say people won't be religious, won't attend church services, won't believe in Jesus and the Bible. It clearly implies that they *will* do these things: they will retain a "form of godliness." But they will, at the very same time, deny God's power to rule in their lives.

What are we to make of all this? What in the world is going on? What is God up to? Ralph Martin, a longtime leader in the charismatic renewal, sums it up best. He says that the churches' "loss of youth, lack of converts, diminished spiritual power, lack of spiritual life among its people, and exodus of leaders from ministry, are all manifestations of God's judgment."

We cannot come to grips with all that is happening around us, and we cannot stay in step with the continuing action of God's Spirit, until we arrive at the realization that God is bringing his righteous judgment upon the world and upon the churches. God's judgment is the only lens through which we can see and comprehend the situation in which we find ourselves.

God's intention in this urgent hour is to bring progressive judgment on our society in a way that drives people to the foot of the Cross. From there he wants to provide for their subsequent care and training by incorporating them into churches that express authentic New Testament Christianity.

Moreover, beyond bringing unbelievers to turn to him, God's judgment is also intended to propel believers out of complacency and into his purpose for their generation. That purpose is the restoration of his church: the return of all that has been lost and the removal of everything that is unbiblical and that undermines Christian truth, life, and mission. All of this is in order to effectively reach the world with the gospel of our Lord Jesus Christ. *This is the divine appointment God has for our generation.* The question is, will we keep our appointment and fulfill our destiny as the people of God?

"If the bugle gives an indistinct sound, who will get ready for battle?" (1 Cor 14:8). I believe that the bugle is anything but indistinct. It is crystal clear. The Spirit of God is sounding an urgent call, so that all may hear and understand our generation's divine appointment in this period of history.

The purpose of God in our time is not the mere renewal of some aspects of familiar American church life but the complete restoration of glorious New Testament Christianity. Sound radical? It is. But it's utterly biblical. Restoration of the church isn't just another good idea. It is God's battle plan for the establishment of his kingdom and the destruction of the domain of Satan at the end of the age.

Earlier I spoke of the terrible slaughter of the unborn that continues in our country because of legalized abortion. I cannot help but think that this has significance in terms of God's action in our day. Satan has set out to thwart other major moves of God at other points in history through the barbaric slaughter of children. When God was preparing Moses as a deliverer for his people, Pharaoh destroyed scores of children in a vain attempt to protect his rule. Centuries later, when God sent Jesus Christ as the deliverer for the whole world, Herod destroyed innocent children in an attempt to block the work of God.

I believe that God is once again raising up a deliverer for his people: the glorious, restored church at the end of the age. Could it be that Satan, once more, is attempting to frustrate God's plans by destroying unborn children, whom God has chosen to fulfill his purposes in this hour? Yet just as Satan failed to extinguish the lives of Moses and of Jesus, so will he fail to extinguish the restoration of God's church.

God is preparing his people in seeming obscurity for a powerful visitation of his Spirit, in which they will shine as lights in the darkness. "For behold, darkness shall cover the earth and gross darkness the peoples. But the Lord shall arise upon thee and his glory shall be seen upon thee, and the Gentiles shall come to thy light and kings to the brightness of thy rising" (Is 60:2-3).

Resistance shall surely come, but God will use even this to unite his church and build strength of conviction in his people. The greater the opposition, the greater the opportunity for God's glory to shine through his restored church.

What a time to be alive! What a time to be in Christ, part of his plan, moving under the guidance and in the power of his Spirit to effectively evangelize the nations, pursuing the divine appointment set before us as members of this most critical generation.

It was in view of just such a time that Peter asked, "What sort of persons ought you to be, therefore, in lives of holiness and godliness, waiting for and hastening the coming of the day of God?" (see 2 Pt 3:11-12). It is a good question. Before we look ahead to see what the church of the future, the fully restored New Testament church, will be like, let's look first at what kind of men and women we must be as we move ahead in God's plan.

TWELVE

The Time Has Come

A S WE LOOK UPON THE MORAL DECAY that runs rampant in our society, as we see the confusion and compromise that afflicts so many Christian bodies, as we witness God's progressive judgment on the world and the church, what are we to do? How are we to respond?

Theologian Carl Henry has said it is time for faithful Christians to stand in "a bold and majestic witness to the holy commandments of God."

The late Francis Schaeffer called on believers to "pay the price of commitment in our sphere of responsibility, regardless of what that price may be."

God has told us in his word that the last days will witness a period of ever-deepening darkness over the nations and, at the same time, an ever-increasing light over his true church (see Is 60). Days of trouble are tailor-made for Christians. In a bankrupt system in which people have exhausted the spectrum of sin, God is preparing his bride.

The Holy Spirit is using the current situation in our society and in the church to bring together Christians of authentic biblical faith. He is sifting out those who play religious games for personal benefit. He is setting the backdrop against which his glorious church can arise in purity and power.

Remember the book, *Satan Is Alive and Well on Planet Earth*? The title is only half true. Satan is alive, all right, but he certainly is not well! "He knows his time is short" (Rv 12:12) as he sees God fashion in obscurity his triumphant church to hasten the Lord Jesus' return so that he can crush Satan under his heel. God's people are destined to end this age not in defeat but in victory, as the most influential people on the face of the earth!

Not all will be converted, but they will be confronted. Not everyone will like us, but they will have to respect us. Not everyone will agree with us, but they will have to deal with us.

I believe God is currently speaking three words to all believers who "have ears to hear":

1. *It is time for us to share God's righteous anger.*

Someone once challenged me: "You know it's a sin to be angry about things God isn't angry about. But did you ever think it a sin *not* to be angry about things God *is* angry about?"

God's anger is mentioned more than 500 times in the Bible. The Greek word for it has as its root meaning, "breathing heavily; passionate." It speaks of something felt deeply because of a deep commitment to holiness. It is a righteous indignation, a holy hatred for sin. Dr. James Orr calls it "the zeal of God for the maintenance of his holiness and honor."

But may a Christian legitimately get angry?

He not only *may*, in some situations he *must*. Ephesians 4:26 says, "Be angry but sin not." This is a command! It is not an excuse for outbursts of temper but a biblical basis for expressing, with a right spirit, the holy anger of God.

The Bible gives us many examples of holy men experiencing God's holy anger. Here is how Paul responded to the intellectual, moral, and spiritual decadence of Athens: "His spirit was grieved and roused to anger as he saw the city was full of idols" (Acts 17:16). David said, "Burning indignation has seized me because of the wicked who forsake thy law" (Ps 119:53). It is written of Jesus that he "loved righteousness and hated wickedness" (Heb 1:9).

Even as Jesus angrily drove out those corrupting God's temple, so must we today angrily oppose those forces attempting to desecrate the new temple of God, the church. To remain silent or apathetic is to be unfaithful. God's call to us, as we feel what he is feeling, is not to launch out hastily in a personal crusade but to ask God to show us his strategy and, with hearts baptized in love, to link arms with other believers to do battle with spiritual powers in the heavenlies.

2. *It is time to acknowledge our dissatisfaction with inadequate church life as we have known it.*

As our hearts become inflamed with a vision for the church as God intends it to be, we are ruined for the stale status quo. We are no longer able to accept mediocrity. We are willing to go wherever we have to go and to do whatever we have to do to partake of authentic New Testament Christianity.

What does this authentic New Testament church life look like? I believe the following twelve characteristics are the essential earmarks of a solid, biblically based church:

1. Jesus is exalted as the Son of God, risen from the dead and reigning as Lord of the universe (Acts 2:22-24).

2. The Bible is honored and taught with authority as God's revealed will for his creation (2 Tm 3:16).

3. There is freedom and vitality in praise and worship (Col 3:17; Ps 150).

4. Genuine love finds practical expression through regular serving, showing honor, and extending hospitality (Jn 13:34-35).

5. People develop deep friendships and foster a sense of family in their midst (Acts 2:42-47; 5:42).

6. There is an emphasis on commitment, not convenience, in the common life of the people (Acts 2:42-47).

7. Leaders place a high priority on pastoral care and do not shrink from exercising biblical authority (1 Pt 5:2; Heb 13:17).

8. Leaders exemplify Christian virtue (integrity, loyalty, humility), not just "charismatic" speaking ability divorced from character (1 Tm 3:1-13).

9. The gift ministries established in the church to aid our

growth to maturity are acknowledged and allowed to operate freely: apostles, prophets, pastors, evangelists, and teachers (Eph 4:11-15).

10. There is an outward evangelistic thrust to reach others with the good news of Jesus Christ (Mt 28:19-20).

11. There is an atmosphere of reality and relevance, not merely of religious ritual (2 Tm 3:5).

12. People's lives have been visibly changed for the better because of their involvement (Rm 12:2).

These twelve essentials are not written only in the Bible, they are also written in our hearts. Somehow we know deep within that God's intention is that we be able to find our place in a church embodying these characteristics and that this is not optional but essential. We may already be experiencing blessing from other Christian involvements: participating in a Bible study, a prayer and praise meeting, a small home fellowship group, a parachurch organization, an evangelistic ministry, even a traditional religious service. And yet somehow we sense that there's more, that we mustn't let these involvements deflect us from pressing on to the unspeakable blessings of relationship and commitment in a body of believers expressing the fullness of authentic New Testament Christianity.

Desperate times require desperate action. In the same passage where Paul warns Timothy that the last days will be filled with "lovers of self, lovers of money, haters of good," those who are "proud, arrogant, abusive," who are "lovers of pleasure rather than lovers of God," who "hold the form of religion but deny the power of it," he offers clear advice on how to relate to them: "Have nothing to do with such people" (see 2 Tm 3:1-5).

Sometimes God *does* call us to "hang tough" in difficult situations, where we are able to advance God's cause and help turn things around. But at other times God's call to us requires that we move on.

Our God is a God of newness. His New Covenant speaks of receiving new wine in new wineskins, having a new heart, being given a new name, singing a new song, proclaiming a new and living way. "Remember not the former things, nor consider the things of old," God reminds us through the prophet Isaiah. "Behold, I am doing a new thing. Now it springs forth; do you not perceive it?" (Is 43:19).

While we must guard ourselves against the trivializing of the Greeks, who "spent their time in nothing except telling or hearing something new" (Acts 17:21), our lives are nevertheless to be characterized by a pioneering spirit that seeks to "keep in step with the Spirit" (Gal 5:25) and to move, as the Israelites did in the desert, behind God's pillar of fire.

God has called us to be pioneers, not settlers. A settler is one who stays put. A pioneer is a person or group that originates or helps open up a new line of thought or action; a trailblazer; a champion of a new order; an advance agent who breaks new ground. This kind of life can only be lived by faith, since our human tendency is always to go with what is safe, familiar, comfortable. As someone has said, "You never learn faith in comfortable surroundings."

Scripture offers many examples of men and women who failed to continue as pioneers and instead stagnated as settlers.

Consider the Israelites, who took more than forty years in the wilderness to complete a journey that could have been made in eleven days. Instead of pressing onward in step with the pillar of cloud by day and the pillar of flame by night, they dragged their heels, grumbled, and longed for the security and familiarity of their former life. As a result, almost none of those who began the journey entered into their inheritance.

Even Moses failed to listen to the ongoing voice of God. On one occasion he was told to strike a rock in order to bring forth water (Ex 17:6). Later, he was told to *speak* to the rock (Nm 20:8), but he instead settled into the former way of operating and pounded the rock with his staff. He thought he could just keep doing what God had told him to do years before. The result: he, too, did not enter into his inheritance.

Jonathan, son of Saul, was to sit at David's right hand when David achieved his kingdom. But when Saul lost God's anointing, Jonathan failed to make a clean break with him and to give himself fully to David. He settled in, turning back to his father's house. Not only did he lose his inheritance alongside David, he also died a tragic and untimely death alongside Saul.

We are told that King Hezekiah pleased God when he "broke in pieces the bronze serpent that Moses had made" (see 2 Kg 18). Why would this please God? Hadn't God used the bronze serpent to bring miraculous healing to the Jews (see Nm 21)? He had indeed; but now, years later, the people had settled in and were clinging to the bronze rod ("The people of Israel burned incense to it; it was called *Nehustan,* or 'piece of bronze'") rather than pressing on with God.

We see the same phenomenon in the New Testament. On the Mount of Transfiguration, we see Peter trying to erect a monument to God's action. We are the same way. We find it so much easier to pitch camp than to press on! The temptation to become settlers rather than pioneers is always with us.

Many of us, for example, have faced this phenomenon head-on in our own personal experience of spiritual renewal. It looks something like this:

Decision. After having routinely attended a religious service on Sunday morning for many years, we recognize a serious deficiency in our Christian life. We yield our life to Christ and are subsequently baptized in the Holy Spirit.

Discovery. We find a whole new way of life in God's Spirit. The Bible comes alive. Prayer meetings and large conferences become a highlight of our life. The adventure of sharing our faith is characterized by great fervor.

Digging In. Highly motivated and idealistic, we settle in to bloom where we are planted. Our vision is nothing less than total conquest: "My church . . . my parish . . . my city . . . my region . . . will be totally renewed! I just know God will do it!"

Disillusionment. Three or five or ten years down the road, we find our zeal waning as burnout starts to set in. We see attendance dwindling at prayer meetings and conferences.

Encouragements to "just get back to basics and things will be like they were in the good old days" sound increasingly hollow. We begin to ask ourselves, "What's gone wrong? Why didn't things catch fire?"

Dilemma. At this point, we go in one of three directions:

—Some resist the leading of the Spirit to press on to the next item on God's agenda. This *disobedience* ultimately leads to *deception*: "Maybe it was all just psychological." "There's no reason not to get into some of these things I used to think were so wrong. After all, God still loves me."

—Others sense God tugging at their hearts, but instead of responding wholeheartedly they shrink back. In time, they *drift* into *depression*: "Why can't things be like they used to be?" "After all the hours I gave to so many of those people, now they aren't even around anymore. Why should I keep knocking myself out?"

—Still others of us are not content to throw in the towel. We sense an urgency in the air: God getting things ready for a final visitation. Knowing that "God is up to something," we commit ourselves to following him wherever he leads. It is this *determination* that catapults us into our *destiny*. "Who knows if we have come into the kingdom for just such a time as this?" (see Est 4:14).

When a space shuttle is launched, the sky is set ablaze by the first-stage booster rockets that propel the aircraft through the earth's atmosphere. When these rockets have finished their task, they fall away into the sea. If they don't, the mission cannot succeed: the spacecraft cannot attain orbit carrying those huge tanks.

I believe that God has used the charismatic renewal of the past twenty years in a similar way: like a mighty booster rocket, it has propelled millions of men and women into new life in the Spirit. Now, as this essential phase winds down, God is readying the next stage, preparing to launch us into the restoration of his church so we can fulfill the Great Commission to reach the world with the gospel. The challenge before us is clear: we must continue forward as pioneers, or we will surely stagnate as settlers.

We need to be like the wise scribes described by Jesus in Matthew 13:52: "Every scribe who has been trained for the kingdom of heaven is like a householder who brings out of his treasure what is new and what is old." Aware that the church is in a transitional period, we must appreciate what God has done in the past. But at the same time, we must not fail to acknowledge what he is saying in the present. We stand at a critical juncture in history, a juncture between the achievements of the past and the awesome potential of the future. If we are going to make every day a masterpiece for God, we mustn't miss our divine appointment!

3. *One final directive that many believe God is currently speaking to those who "have ears to listen" is: It is time to recognize our need for a supportive environment in which to live out our Christian convictions in the midst of a hostile society.*

In this fragmented society, where people cry out for meaningful relationships, God intends his people to enjoy the stability of genuine Christian community. Times of difficulty are preparing Christians to become more responsibly related to one another.

We need to be committed to a functioning local body in which the priority is on building relationships, not just on attending meetings. With the pressures of a pagan culture increasing, we will not be able to survive as individuals or families, much less flourish, unless we are knit together with others who also want to live uncompromisingly for the Lord. I believe we will not be able to stand for God's cause unless we are as devoted to one another as were the Christians depicted in the Acts of the Apostles. Then, as a people and not merely as isolated individuals, will we be able to pray intelligently, pursue Spirit-inspired strategies, and march through this time of judgment as a mighty and victorious army.

I believe that God is indeed raising up a new breed of men and women in our day who are pioneers, not settlers. Unwilling to settle in, they are hoisting their sails and moving where the Spirit is blowing. They are willing to remain fluid, to learn new things and unlearn old things, so that outdated traditions and preconceived notions will not hinder them. Consumed with a passion to please God and to reject all excuses and compromises, they accept that the phrase "constant change is here to stay" is not a cliche but an accurate description of life in the kingdom of God. They are determined to embrace their divine appointment!

THIRTEEN

The Church of the Future

A S SPIRIT-LED BELIEVERS driven to pursue our divine appointment, both in our personal lives and as members of God's people, we know we can't just sit back and wring our hands over the present weaknesses and failings of the church. Nor may we sit in prideful judgment. Rather, our call is to move on with God and to join him in his revolutionary work of restoring the church so we can reach the world with his glorious gospel.

And God is moving on! I believe we are witnessing, right now, the emergence of the church of the future. God is fashioning in obscurity his instrument for confronting the nations. What has begun as a soft explosion, unnoticed by many, will slowly but surely rock our nation and the world.

In this chapter I would like to outline three earmarks of this church of the future which is even now being unfolded in our midst. Our divine appointment is to obey God and give our lives away to see this New Testament Christianity restored in our day.

Biblical Radicalism

"The vast majority of people who are members of churches in America today are not Christians. I say that without the slightest fear of contradiction. I base it on empirical evidence of twenty-four years of examining tens of thousands of people."

Who said these striking words? Some wild-eyed Christian extremist with a chip on his shoulder? Actually, the statement came from the nationally-known, highly-respected evangelical pastor of the 6,500-member Coral Ridge Presbyterian Church, Dr. D. James Kennedy. He is not being self-righteous but merely honest in saying that many people who call themselves Christians have never genuinely come to repentance and faith. They have never made that radical change in attitude toward themselves and God: "If anyone would come after me, he must deny himself and take up his cross daily and follow me" (Lk 9:23).

Dr. Kennedy isn't the only one who has noticed this phenomenon. A high-ranking leader in the Roman Catholic Church has lamented the fact that "our people have been sacramentalized but not evangelized." That description applied to me during the first twenty years of my life!

A genuine disciple of Jesus Christ *must* be radical. Not radical in the political sense but in the sense of the Latin word it comes from: *radix*, or root. Christians are people who have been changed "from the root." This speaks of an inner transformation so radical that it cannot help but result in changed behavior. This is the kind of change John the Baptist was looking for when he told his hearers to "produce fruit in keeping with repentance" (Mt 3:8).

Jesus meant what he said: "Any of you who does not give up everything he has cannot be my disciple" (Lk 14:33). "Not everyone who says to me, 'Lord, Lord,' will enter the kingdom of heaven, but only he who does the will of my Father who is in heaven" (Mt 7:21).

In his "Summer Street Evangelism Report," David Wilkerson once told of an unusual experience he had during a street rally. Two prostitutes came up to him and asked him to pray for them. "Pray for the Lord's blessing on us," they said. "Pray God will help us to help others, to love people."

Wilkerson asked whether they didn't mean they wanted prayer to be saved and set free from prostitution. He was shocked when they assured him they were already saved! "The Bible says all things are lawful," they explained. "We enjoy what we do, and God wants us to be happy. We are loved, and we love God, too. To the pure, all things are pure. Our minds are pure, and so is our prostitution."

"I could not convince them," Wilkerson later recounted, "that they were sinners, breakers of the commandments of Christ. Someone had sold them on a message of *grace without repentance or separation.*"

Acceptance of Jesus as Savior without acknowledgment of Jesus as Lord never occurs in the New Testament. Today God is calling us to turn from such blindness toward obedience. He wants to purge his church of that most subtle heresy: the offer of salvation without repentance, where people are called to "believe" but not to *obey.* "In the past God overlooked such ignorance, but now he commands all people everywhere to repent" (Acts 17:30).

Coming under the loving lordship of Jesus Christ means an end to our "rights" as well as to our wrongs. It means the end of life on our own terms. Once we see how he has totally given his life on our behalf, how can we give anything less in return?

The church of the future is characterized by biblical radicalism, not empty religious profession. It is composed of uncompromising men and women who are utterly committed to Jesus as their Savior *and* their Lord.

Community Orientation

In his best-selling book *Megatrends,* John Naisbitt observes that "the most reliable way to anticipate the future is by understanding the present."

Today in the United States there are some seventy-eight million men and women between the ages of seventeen and thirty-six. These are the "baby-boomers," the generation born in the years following the Second World War. There are another fifty-four million under the age of seventeen. These 132 million people will set the pace for our society in the 1990s and beyond. As *U.S. News and World Report* recently said, this "richest and best-educated of generations is reshaping almost every aspect of American life from politics to marriage as the children of the social revolution head toward middle age. They are destined to shape the country's cultural landscape for the rest of the century."

The signs of the baby-boomers' influence are everywhere. Realizing that this group is nutrition-conscious, fast-food restaurants are expanding their menus to include more salads and breakfast foods. Hotels and motels are adding jogging tracks, racquetball courts, and whirlpool baths to their facilities to accommodate this generation's interest in physical fitness. Even the Levis people are reshaping their famous jeans to accommodate this group's middle-age spread.

How will the church relate to the baby-boomers? Are we alert to the fact that a generation is emerging on the scene that generally doesn't feel comfortable with the image, music, or jargon of traditional religious life? How are we going to evangelize them?

Jack Sims, one of the foremost Christian authorities on the baby-boom generation, says this group is looking for "an emphasis on biblical living, not mere biblical talking. Churches that intend to minister to people under thirty-six must understand their lack of interest in religion as it is being presented to them today. Churches that fail to effectively communicate with them will die slow deaths as their manpower and money dry up."

Today people are being driven ever further from one another as the family breaks down, society becomes ever more mobile, neighborhoods evaporate, and the pace of life grows increasingly frantic. Mass escape into the world of videos and cable programming only makes the problem worse.

Yet deep inside all of us there remains the yearning for something real and meaningful in relationships. The generation of the sixties' radicals that not so long ago marched in demonstrations and discussed society's ills in smoke- and music-filled college dorm rooms is still uneasy, still searching for reality. They seek a sense of belonging, friendship, acceptance, love. Yet they are becoming increasingly insecure and withdrawn, as these basic relational experiences elude them, remaining just beyond their grasp.

The Madison Avenue moguls who produce television commercials are aware of this hunger. They invite us to "reach out and touch someone" and show people engaged in heart-warming long-distance phone calls, all to soaring violin accompaniment. Starry-eyed couples nestle before a glowing fireplace, inhaling the spiraling steam from mugs of fresh-brewed coffee. A crowd of friends at the bar turns en masse to toast someone's long-awaited arrival: it's Miller time!

It all looks so inviting. But, if anything, it increases people's heartache over the drabness of their own daily reality. "Why isn't it like that for me?"

God wants to supply our basic human relational needs—in reality, not just in theory—through his church. His purpose from the beginning was for us to experience a different quality of life in a spiritual family. "God sets the solitary in families," says the psalmist (Ps 68:6). It is from this nurturing base that we are to evangelize the world; it is into this spiritual family that we are to incorporate them.

People today are looking not just for religious services and entertaining preaching, but for a way of life in which people are concretely concerned for one another. The church of the future is a caring, committed community, not just an unconnected crowd of people.

Thus leaders must be careful how they build (1 Cor 3:10). There is a big difference between attracting an audience and building the church, between blessing people and building them together as living stones (Eph 2:22). As someone has said, "God is not so concerned with how quickly we build as with how well we build."

Arthur Wallis, a prophetic leader from Great Britain, has noted that "Community is not just another thing recovered by the charismatic movement. It is the very essence of the church and the very lifestyle of the kingdom."

The church God is restoring is marked by caring, sharing, and bearing. Amid a fragmented society, Christians are developing a community mentality. We enjoy a form of extended family, in which we learn together to be supportive of, and accountable to, one another.

In my experience, I have seen this embodied in a lifestyle in which leaders function as friends first and co-workers second; relationships are based on commitment, not mere convenience; people nurture their relationships in small groupings, both structured and spontaneous; singles support each other through vulnerable years by cultivating healthy friendships or even living together in "brothers" or "sisters" households; children are raised in a godly environment (often including a Christian school); couples are committed to caring for each other so that no one feels alone in coping with marital problems, raising children, or handling finances.

Brothers and sisters joyfully serve one another: helping a family move, taking meals to one who is ill or who has just given birth, fixing a car, devising a budget, raking leaves—you name it. All this enables them to evangelize from a posture of demonstration, not mere declaration.

Does all this sound vaguely familiar? Like something you have read about in your Bible? You will find it in the book of Acts. Those early Christians, with their radical community lifestyle, made an impact on the world around them. They were a force to be reckoned with, not a farce to be ridiculed.

The baby-boomers, so many of whom are turned off by traditional church life, can be powerfully attracted by seeing this brand of Christianity in action. This kind of community orientation will enable us once again to arrest the attention of a watching world.

Prophetic Involvement

Thank you all for coming to our 11 A.M. service. Special thanks to Grandma Gilligan for filling in at the pump organ. I hope you all had a good time and feel really blessed. I'm sorry we went five minutes over our noon deadline. Remember that prayer meeting is cancelled until further notice. Don't forget our covered-dish supper Friday. I hope you can make it. If not, the missus and I look forward to seeing you next Sunday morning. I'll be continuing my six-month series on "Being a Nice Person." Have a nice day!

Not exactly the church triumphant, is it? In recent generations, Christians have retreated from involvement in society at large, preferring to settle down in pseudo-spiritual ghettos, seeking shelter from the world. They may reach a point where the world no longer influences them much. But they also reach a point where they no longer influence the world at all. God's prophetic voice becomes muted, if not choked off altogether. And in the course of losing its societal relevance, the church loses its spiritual relevance as well.

God is emphasizing our call to be a prophetic people and to speak with a prophetic voice to our society. As in earlier days, when God raised up an individual prophet to proclaim the word of the Lord on issues of righteousness and justice, so today he is awakening the "sleeping giant"—his church—to come out of the pews and to address, compassionately but without compromise, the concerns of his heart.

Our role as the "salt of the earth" (Mt 5:13) is to preserve and extend God's justice, and to do battle with the "spiritual forces of evil in the heavenly realms" (Eph 6:12). In our posture as spiritual warriors, we must boldly set a course of action as God reveals his strategy for conquest. This is not mere political involvement or activism, it is the church mobilizing its people and utilizing its resources to bring God's will to pass "on earth as it is in heaven."

American Christians have walked away from a spiritual heritage that was instrumental in shaping the content and structure of our culture and government. Millions are being tragically duped by secular humanist thought that sees coincidence rather than providence in the birth of our nation. Many have been deceived into thinking that religious belief and morality were never meant to influence government and politics. Yet to accept this view requires an almost total disregard for American history and desertion of the guiding principles of our forefathers.

Christopher Columbus set out to discover the New World not in a quest for fame or treasure but out of a prophetic and evangelistic stirring that came from prayer and Scripture meditation. In his diary he recorded his motivation:

> It was the Lord who put it into my mind. I could feel his hand upon me . . . there is no question the inspiration was from the Holy Spirit because he comforted me with rays of marvelous illumination from the holy Scriptures . . . . No one should fear to undertake any task in the name of our Savior if it is just and if the intention is purely for his holy service. The gospel must still be preached to so many lands in such a short time. This is what convinces me.

The Mayflower Compact explains why the Pilgrims came to America: "Having undertaken for the glory of God and the advancement of the Christian faith. . . ."

The first governor of the Plymouth colony, William Bradford, echoed the Pilgrims' vision in stating that they came "for propagating and advancing the gospel of the kingdom of Christ in these remote parts of the world."

The first schools in America were conducted in churches. The first textbook was the Bible. The first teachers were pastors. Three of America's oldest and most respected universities—Harvard, Yale, and Princeton—were founded to train leaders for Christian ministry. Harvard stated in her "Rules and Precepts" in 1642: "Let every student be plainly instructed and earnestly pressed to consider well the main end of his life and studies is to know God and Jesus Christ which is eternal life (Jn 17:5) and therefore to lay Christ in the bottom as the only foundation of all knowledge and learning."

In the rotunda of the Capitol building in Washington, D.C., is a painting of the Pilgrims in which Captain Brewster sits with an open Bible on his lap. Clearly visible are the words, "The New Testament according to our Lord and Savior Jesus Christ." On the sail of the ship in the background is the motto, "In God We Trust."

In the U.S. Supreme Court, above the chair of the Chief Justice, are printed the Ten Commandments, with the great American Eagle protecting them.

How have we strayed so far from our spiritual roots?

The church's restoration in our day consists of men and women who want to do their part to restore a complete view of our nation's spiritual heritage, so that our future can be one in which traditional, biblical, Judeo-Christian values can flourish. We are not confusing America with the kingdom of God or naively saying that all our forefathers were Christians. We don't envision Jesus seated at the Father's right hand waving an American flag and humming "The Star-Spangled Banner." But we do acknowledge that our nation's early settlers had a prophetic vision, that our nation has a rich spiritual heritage, and that we have a legitimate and important voice in shaping the future of our society.

The church of the future will no longer remain ignorant of its prophetic role. We are being stirred by the Spirit to speak out and act in the cause of truth and righteousness in every area of public life, not just during election years but all the time. We must speak and act concerning neglect of the poor, homosexuality, secular humanism in the schools, abortion, infanticide, euthanasia, pornography, and legislation destructive of the family. As Bible teacher Bill Gothard says, "The pulpit, not the media, is to be the most powerful voice in our land."

The Challenge

I believe there has never before been a day like this in the history of the church. After centuries of ignorance, darkness, and paralysis, the Holy Spirit is working to restore a church marked by biblical radicalism, community orientation, and prophetic involvement, to prepare the Bride for the return of her Bridegroom. God's original intention, to "present her to himself as a radiant church without stain or wrinkle or any other blemish, but holy and blameless" (Eph 5:27), is not mere wishful thinking. It is becoming a present reality more and more with each day that passes. "Some of the wise will stumble, so that they may be refined, purified, and made spotless until the time of the end, for it will still come at the *appointed* time" (Dn 11:35).

We must not mistakenly think that the refining and purifying that must be done to produce a spotless church will be easy. It will challenge even "the wise." Yet this, too, is part of our divine appointment in these end times.

Are you ready to link arms with others who, in the spirit of Peter, Paul, and Stephen, reject the spirit of compromise and stand courageously for living out the word of God? The call of God is growing clearer each day, but only the obedient can hear it.

Today, those who "have ears to hear" are joyfully responding to the call God is giving our generation. Recognizing that their personal conversion catapults them into a new dimension where divine appointments are a way of life, they are throwing off shackles of fear and unbelief to seize their destiny and make every day a masterpiece for God. They are aggressively stepping out in personal evangelism, moving in the miraculous, and sustaining it all through a rich prayer base of regular, intimate communion with God.

As we respond to God and fulfill our divine appointment in this generation for the restoration of that sleeping giant known as the church to evangelize the world, we will understand the loud shout that Jesus releases upon his return (see 1 Thes 4:16). Surely excitement will explode in his heart as he rends the heavens to fulfill *his* divine appointment with his bride, his glorious church, restored to his original intentions, fulfilling his purposes. Would we want to present him with anything less?

Hurry! Your appointment is waiting!

Appendix

A Sample Personal Tract— Doris Tomczak

A FEW MOMENTS AGO WE MET, but we really didn't have much time to talk. If we had, I would have enjoyed sharing with you a little of my life story and the wonderful transformation that took place almost ten years ago. Do you believe that a person's whole destiny can be permanently altered in a matter of minutes? 10:30 P.M. on March 13, 1972 marked that moment for me. I've never been the same since!

"Insecure" is the word that best describes my state prior to March of 1972. I grew up feeling "lost in the crowd"—being one of eight children and for eight years attending an overcrowded Catholic grade school. I was born with an introverted personality anyway, and being publicly humiliated several times by the teachers at school only deepened my insecurities and fear of people.

My poor self-image continued to worsen in high school, as I compared my beauty, talents, and popularity with the other girls and always seemed to come up short. Why did I have to have thin, lifeless hair? A crooked front tooth? Big shoulders? Why wasn't I given an outgoing, bubbly personality like the cheerleaders I so envied, or an intellect like my straight-A sister? The longer I looked in the mirror, the more depressed and bitter I got. "God, *you* blew it! *You* made me this way. You didn't give me a fair deal. Thanks anyway, but I won't be needing any more of your 'loving care' in my life!"

At seventeen, I began to direct my bitterness and inner rebellion toward my parents. I felt I'd already been cheated in life by God, so who were they to put any further restrictions on my happiness? "Who says I have to go to church? It's meaningless anyway. Who says I can't stay out all night if I want? Who says I can't smoke dope and do as I want sexually?"

Upon entering college, my looks took a turn for the better, and I suddenly found myself one of the girls most sought after by the fraternity guys. At last I was pretty and popular. But I was compromising the moral standard I'd been raised with. I would do anything it took to cover up the low self-esteem and insecurity I knew was inside. The guilt and frustration I lived with were simply projected on my parents in the form of anger and hatred. When my mother began to fear for her life when left alone in the house with me, my father asked me to move out. My bad influence on my younger brothers and sisters also brought him to make that decision.

On my own, it took only nine months to realize that my "freedom" was destroying me from the inside out. The increasing guilt could only temporarily be numbed by partying, bar-hopping, alcohol, cigarettes, food, or a "fling" with a new guy. Deep inside I was depressed, even though outwardly I did my best to cover it up. I knew the depression and loneliness would simply carry over into later life unless I did something. Valium wasn't helping—it only made things worse. I was becoming hard and calloused in my conscience and tried to convince myself that "there is no God, after all." I felt less guilt if I thought there would be no one to answer to. But alone at night there was a small part of me that knew he existed and reminded me I was not right with him.

Something finally happened to me that changed my entire life. It began when I noticed a change in my parents. Mom was no longer complaining about all her aches and pains, and Dad was more warm and affectionate toward her. They were smiling more. When I asked what was going on, they said they had just given Jesus Christ complete control of their lives and that he was changing them from the inside out. They said they were experiencing a whole new life.

No one knew better than I that a new life was exactly what I needed, too. So I cautiously agreed to go with them to a meeting, to learn more about what they were experiencing. Once there, I couldn't help but notice a real love among the people, and the joy they were experiencing was greater than anything I'd ever seen in the singles bars. I was jealous. Several young people told how their lives had been dramatically transformed when they gave Jesus Christ control of their lives. They talked about him as if they really knew him—as though he were a real person who loved them and was intimately involved in their daily lives!

I wanted that, but I also wanted to maintain control of my life. I wasn't quite ready. What if Jesus showed me I needed to make some major shifts in my lifestyle? What if he told me some relationships would have to be changed? What would I have left? I wrestled with my decision for six weeks.

Finally, I realized that Jesus was not "religion." He was drawing me into a *relationship* with himself, to free me of my guilt, forgive me, and start me on a whole new path in life. Certainly I had botched it up enough trying to run it apart from him. So on March 13, 1972, at 10:30 P.M., I repented of running my own selfish life and asked Jesus Christ to "take the controls" and make me the kind of woman he wanted me to be.

I immediately sensed God's presence with me, for the first time in my life. A peace settled upon me that I'd never known, and I felt totally clean. And that was just the beginning!

The next day I was reconciled with my parents and within a month I was living back home. The former tension slowly but surely lifted from our home as, one by one, my brothers and sisters put their lives under the lordship of Jesus Christ. The radical change in my life paved the way for them. We were a new family, experiencing a fondness and care for each other and communicating as we never had before. Selfishness was vanishing as we were now learning to obey God's will (expressed in the Bible) rather than our own. We suddenly had the power to turn away from our selfish habits and found ourselves enjoying life.

That was almost ten years ago. Since then, Jesus has delivered me from low self-esteem and has given me a new purpose for living. I genuinely *like* the woman I've become. He has also given me a tremendous Christian husband and four delightful children. Now our lives are involved in introducing others to the person of Jesus Christ and then helping them mature in their faith. We couldn't be happier! Life is now an adventure instead of drudgery.

How about you? As you were reading this, did you find yourself identifying with some of the things I said? Do you find you've reached a point in your own life where you realize you can't go on anymore as you are, but that you need a complete change from the inside out? Scores of people all over the world are cutting through religious counterfeits and finding reality in committing their lives totally to Jesus Christ. I want to challenge you in this same direction. Know that it is no coincidence or accident that you hold this little leaflet in your hands.

Here's how you can take your first step. Be assured, it *is* possible to start again! (Here the writer can state clearly and concisely the steps to begin a new life in Jesus Christ.)

People of Destiny, a bimonthly magazine edited by Larry Tomczak, is for Christians who know they have a vital part to play in reaching this world for Jesus Christ. If that's you, *People of Destiny* magazine is a tool for your hands. It tackles those tough issues you need to know:

- discover your gifts and fulfill your ministry;
- overcome sinful habits and live victoriously;
- become more effective and disciplined in prayer and Bible Study;
- develop strong committed relationships;
- believe God for signs and wonders to confirm the preaching of his Word;
- speak out with conviction on the moral issues of our day;
- learn how to play a vital part in the restoration of New Testament Christianity and the evangelization of the world.

"You can discover your destiny in life! Our commitment to help you is not simply a preference; it's a passion."
—Larry Tomczak

For more information write:

People of Destiny
P.O. Box 2335
Wheaton, Maryland 20902

Exciting titles
by Myles Munroe

IN PURSUIT OF PURPOSE

Best-selling author Myles Munroe reveals here the key to personal fulfillment: purpose. We must pursue purpose because our fulfillment in life depends upon our becoming what we were born to be and do. *In Pursuit of Purpose* will guide you on that path to finding purpose.
ISBN 1-56043-103-2 $9.99p

UNDERSTANDING YOUR POTENTIAL

This is a motivating, provocative look at the awesome potential trapped within you, waiting to be realized. This book will cause you to be uncomfortable with your present state of accomplishment and dissatisfied with resting on your past success.
ISBN 1-56043-046-X $9.99p

RELEASING YOUR POTENTIAL

Here is a complete, integrated, principles-centered approach to releasing the awesome potential trapped within you. If you are frustrated by your dreams, ideas, and visions, this book will show you a step-by-step pathway to releasing your potential and igniting the wheels of purpose and productivity.
ISBN 1-56043-072-9 $9.99p

MAXIMIZING YOUR POTENTIAL

Are you bored with your latest success? Maybe you're frustrated at the prospect of retirement. This book will refire your passion for living! Learn to maximize the God-given potential lying dormant inside you through the practical, integrated, and penetrating concepts shared in this book. Go for the max—die empty!
ISBN 1-56043-105-9 $9.99p

Available at your local Christian bookstore.

Internet: http://www.reapernet.com

D *Destiny Image*
New Releases

Destiny Image
New Releases

ENCOUNTERS WITH A SUPERNATURAL GOD
by Jim and Michal Ann Goll.
The Golls know that angels are real. They have firsthand experience with supernatural angelic encounters. Go on an adventure with Jim and Michal Ann and find out if God has a supernatural encounter for you!
ISBN 1-56043-199-7 $9.99p

THE LOST ART OF INTERCESSION
by Jim W. Goll.
How can you experience God's anointing power as a result of your own prayer? Learn what the Moravians discovered during their 100-year prayer Watch. They sent up prayers; God sent down His power. Jim Goll, who ministers worldwide through a teaching and prophetic ministry, urges us to heed Jesus' warning to "watch." Through Scripture, the Moravian example, and his own prayer life, Jim Goll proves that "what goes up must come down."
ISBN 1-56043-697-2 $9.99p

WORSHIP: THE PATTERN OF THINGS IN HEAVEN
by Joseph L. Garlington, Sr.
Joseph Garlington, a favorite Promise Keepers' speaker and worship leader, delves into Scripture to reveal worship and praise from a Heaven's-eye view. Learn just how deep, full, and anointed God intends our worship to be.
ISBN 1-56043-195-4 $9.99p

USER FRIENDLY PROPHECY
by Larry J. Randolph.
Hey! Now you can learn the basics of prophecy and how to prophesy in a book that's written for you! Whether you're a novice or a seasoned believer, this book will stir up the prophetic gift God placed inside you and encourage you to step out in it.
ISBN 1-56043-695-6 $9.99p

Available at your local Christian bookstore.
Internet: http://www.reapernet.com

D *Destiny Image*
New Releases

D *Destiny Image*
Revival Books
by Dr. Michael L. Brown

THE END OF THE AMERICAN GOSPEL ENTERPRISE
In this important and confrontational book, Dr. Michael Brown identifies the sore spots of American Christianity and points out the prerequisites for revival.
ISBN 1-56043-002-8 $8.99p

FROM HOLY LAUGHTER TO HOLY FIRE
America is on the edge of a national awakening—God is responding to the cries of His people! This stirring book passionately calls us to remove the roadblocks to revival. If you're looking for the "real thing" in God, this book is must reading! (A revised edition of *High-Voltage Christianity*.)
ISBN 1-56043-181-4 $9.99p

HOW SAVED ARE WE?
This volume clearly challenges us to question our born-again experience if we feel no call to personal sacrifice, separation from the world, and the hatred of sin. It will create in you the desire to live a life truly dedicated to God.
ISBN 1-56043-055-9 $8.99p

IT'S TIME TO ROCK THE BOAT
Here is a book whose time has come. It is a radical, noncompromising, no-excuse call to genuine Christian activism: intercessory prayer and the action that one must take as a result of that prayer.
ISBN 1-56043-106-7 $9.99p

WHATEVER HAPPENED TO THE POWER OF GOD
Why are the seriously ill seldom healed? Why do people fall in the Spirit yet remain unchanged? Why can believers speak in tongues and wage spiritual warfare without impacting society? This book confronts you with its life-changing answers.
ISBN 1-56043-042-7 $9.99p

Available at your local Christian bookstore.
Internet: http://www.reapernet.com

Destiny Image
Favorites

FROM THE FATHER'S HEART
by Charles Slagle.
This is a beautiful look at the Father's heart. This sensitive selection includes short love notes and letters, as well as prophetic words from God to those among His children who diligently seek Him. Be ready for a time with God as you read this book.
ISBN 0-914903-82-9 $8.99p

DIDN'T YOU READ MY BOOK?
by Dr. Richard E. Eby.
This best-selling book is a provocative look at the truths to be found in God's book, written by one who has seen the reality of many of these truths for himself. Dr. Eby has said, "The best possible experience on earth is to converse with Almighty God; the next best is to share His words with others; and third best is to have a reader who is open to hear His truth."
ISBN 1-56043-448-1 $8.99p

THE CROSS IS STILL MIGHTIER THAN THE SWITCHBLADE
by Don Wilkerson.
Don Wilkerson, co-director of the original Brooklyn Teen Challenge with his brother David, tells of the ministry's incredible growth and success in working with troubled youth today. With current eyewitness reports and testimonies of former addicts and gang members, he proves that *The Cross Is Still Mightier Than the Switchblade.*
ISBN 1-56043-264-0 $9.99p

SECRETS OF THE MOST HOLY PLACE
by Don Nori.
Here is a prophetic parable you will read again and again. The winds of God are blowing, drawing you to His Life within the Veil of the Most Holy Place. There you begin to see as you experience a depth of relationship your heart has yearned for. This book is a living, dynamic experience with God!
ISBN 1-56043-076-1 $9.99p

Available at your local Christian bookstore.

Internet: http://www.reapernet.com

Prices subject to change without notice.   3:18